WHAT IS A
Selfish Baby Daddy?

BY: ABLYSS GILLESPIE & ONNEY

PUBLISHED BY:
ONNEY PUBLISHING & PERFORMANCES, INC.

Copyright © 2016
Selfish Subjects, Inc.

ISBN-13: 978-0997312805
ISBN-10: 0997312807
LCCN: 2016905741

Publishing /Editing /Cover Design
By:
Onney Publishing & Performances, Inc.
P.O. Box 309
Missouri City, Texas, 77459
www.onney.net

AUTHORS NOTE:
Names, characters, places and incidents are products of the Authors imagination and are used fictitiously based on testimonies of true events. Any resemblance to actual events, locals or persons, living or dead, is entirely coincidental.

A Word from Our Authors

Ablyss

So many ideas came to mind in the creation of "What is a Selfish Baby Daddy?" As a single mother, I found myself in constant battle with my baby daddy. Some of the arguments would be smooth, but the majority would end in resentment and the creation of enemy territory. Weekend visitations would consist of him handling situations and circumstances the best way he knew how, while I would become truly angry and irate when the little one returned. This led to me picking up the phone sometimes and expressing my feelings in a hurtful way, or long three-to-four day texts that never ended until we both finally ran out of unapologetic words.

As the years went on, many other "Baby Mamas" shared their stories with me and ironically, some of the dialogues were similar. Speaking with these women really helped me to see how the inequality of raising children in separate homes is increasing.

Writing this book spoke to my soul and speaks volumes for me as a single mother doing the job daily by myself. As an author and as a human being, I have grown, and yet I still have a long way to go. But in the end, I am a single mother who will continue to be strong and raise my child to the best of my abilities and do the best I can to set a positive example for many mothers and fathers in the future.

-Ablyss

Onney

*C*oming from a broken home and suffering from being the fatherless child, some of the experiences written in this book I learned first-hand. With the many incidents that occurred, I suffered as a child, not knowing who to blame. There were times that I actually blamed myself for the misfortune of my parents not working out. Seemingly so, history repeated itself when I had my children.

Although unfortunate, I gained much clarity on what my parents couldn't find the words to explain to me as a child. With those experiences, good, bad, and indifferent, I realized that I was not the only mother dealing with the misfortune of a broken home and unhealthy communication with the father of their children. In fact, the statistics have proven that there are more than an acceptable number of these circumstances in all different ethnic backgrounds and social status groups.

With single-parenting increasing at an alarming rate, Ablyss and I decided to write a book to encourage functionality into dysfunctional co-parenting environments. In hopes to bridge the gap in communication, we have chosen to share some of our stories along with stories from others, to bring awareness to all parents, both custodial and non-custodial, single or married, on some of the issues that arise in selfish situations. Could you be one of these parents that are found within these pages? Or

are you on the other end of the scale? Take a read
and see...

-Onney

Preface

*T*he feelings and emotions of not being able to add in the decision-making process and assist in handling in-home decisions is hard on the non-custodial parent; simultaneously, it can consciously or unconsciously create hardships on the custodial parent when doing it all by oneself or not allowing the non-custodial parent to assist. This book explains what the other parent is thinking, even if the comments or expressions may come across as adverse, unfavorable, or contravening. It is in the best interest of the child/children for both parents to maintain healthy communication; if this can't happen, then it is important to seek proper assistance.

Single mothers and fathers are everywhere, and in some cases, both parents truly want what is best for the child or children. Have the following questions and/or statements ever come to mind?

- Why would he/she say this about me? I am a great parent.
- Why would you not want me to spend more time with our child?
- Why does he/she say the meanest things to me?
- What did I do to deserve all of this havoc? I want what is best and I can make sure of this better than he/she.

The above questions can come across as selfish to some, if answered a certain way. One parent can appear selfish based on their past experiences with another parent, family, or just life in general. Which one are you?

- Do I respond the way I do as a defense mechanism?
- Do I handle situations the way I do to hurt the other parent's feelings out of resentment?
- Is it my way or the highway?

Do you really know if you fit the category of being self-indulgent, self-interested, and self-seeking? Does the other parent get you to a point of having to place a guard up? Do you appear to come across as parsimonious, ungenerous, or vain? If you see yourself within these pages, are you able to find the most positive way to correct yourself? If you see yourself within these pages, how can you handle the situation differently?

Some may find this book offensive, some may find it refining and refreshing, while others may just find it practical and helpful. In the end, the child is the most important factor within the equation.

It's on you to figure out if you are, or want to be, the opposite of what's read within these pages. It's up to you as the reader to figure out if benevolence, kindheartedness, or being magnanimous are character traits which you would like to possess, not for the benefit of the other parent, but in the best interest of the child. Some of the expressions in this book may guide parents into being better co-parents. We, as authors, are hoping both parents can and will improve at co-parenting.

"What is a Selfish Baby Daddy?" is geared towards raising awareness on social parenting issues that arise involving mothers whether single, divorced, or married, whether they are raising the children alone or living with the fathers but still feel as if they are doing the job alone. This book will highlight some of the scenarios that cause dysfunctionality in a single and co-parenting environment. We would like to thank all the "Baby Mamas and Baby Daddies" who assisted us in bringing subjects to light and for allowing us to use your stories to ensure the success of this book.

ABOUT THE AUTHORS

ABLYSS

$\mathcal{M}$elanie Wilson, also known as Ablyss Gillespie, was born and raised in Missouri City, Texas, and graduated from Willowridge High School in 1995.

After moving back to Houston from Memphis, Tennessee, life's events encouraged her to express herself through art and music. In 2003, she joined the Houston poetry scene where she met various other artists, collaborated with them, and became truly inspired. This is how she met Lanora Laws, known to the world as Onney.

Ironically, Ablyss was raised one street over from Onney, and they both attended the same high school. Ablyss actually graduated with Onney's brother. On the poetry scene, Ablyss tapped into her skills of playwright. She presented her first play at Catfish Willy's, entitled, "Acceptance Shadow" in front of an audience of dozens over a weekend. Expanding from this excitement, Ablyss decided to continue developing productions. Her second production, "Intimidation vs. Intimidation", was showcased at local restaurants and rental facilities.

Eventually, she decided she wanted to move her productions to black box theaters. While "Intimidation vs. Intimidation" was showing at the legendary Silver House Theater, Ablyss began working with Jonathan Dale Samuels, whom she had met some years before. The CEO of Dahrk Sity Productions, Jonathan, a.k.a Kik-A-Flo, partnered with Ablyss to work on music. Some of his ideas and inspirational styles helped to mold and create a certain essence, which she added to her future productions. Currently, Ablyss uses his style of music and creative beats in all of her stage plays.

After the run of her first play at The Silver House Theatre, she penned another play entitled, "Submission Adultery Disease", and while writing this production, Ablyss hit Kosmic Oasis, a known studio for underground artists owned by K'monte, to record "Mama's Titty", her jazz single. Ablyss desired to do everything on a bigger scale so she held a concert event entitled, "Dusty Records" and there, she let the world in on her singing abilities and surprised everyone with her poetry book entitled "Cycle of Alteration", published by Onney Publishing & Performances, Inc.

Following this success, Ablyss went on to showcase "Submission Adultery Disease" (S.A.D.) at The Silver House Theater. Shortly afterward, Ablyss became pregnant with her daughter, who is autistic. Being a mother takes up most of her time, but she has traveled to New York on several occasions to perform on the legendary SOB stage with Kindred Family and was the opening act for Eric Roberson.

The behavior of Ablyss's daughter became a bit much for her caregivers to handle, so she took a short break from music, theater, and writing to focus on her little one. After getting her daughter where she needed her to be, Ablyss was hired for a Walmart commercial and an Aspire Network commercial.

She also directed the stage play entitled, "Badu-Izms: A Tribute to Erykah Badu", and showcased "Bougie, Broke, and Single", (formerly known as "Intimidation vs. Intimidation") a year later.

During this time, Ablyss also graduated college, receiving her Bachelor's and Master's Degree in Leadership, while minoring in Non-profit Management from Northeastern University online in Boston, Massachusetts. To assist her in understanding the non-profit sector, Ablyss was the President for two years over the Willowridge Mighty Eagle Band Booster Club. While leading the club, she put together various fundraiser talent shows to assist in raising money. Volunteering her time for the booster club was one of the best times of her life. As CEO of Zalyn's Inc.; a company that specializes in event coordinating, Ablyss is happy to continue her love for art, writing, and productions.

ONNEY

$\mathcal{W}$hile the males of the industry continue to dominate, a lesser gratitude is paid to their female counterparts. Along comes Onney, to counter the perception with her no-nonsense demeanor mixed with a spirited personality. As a member of the celebrated Laws family (Ronnie, Hubert, Eloise and Debra), Onney has created a strong following in her career as well.

Onney is a writer and poet who addresses a wide range of life's issues. She is an insightful hip-hop poetess who uses her incendiary vocal skills to take us into the erotica of love and the morass of social and political issues that concern us all. Her observations are laced with wisdom beyond her years and sautéed in humor that holds the listener or the reader rapt.

Although Onney's first love has always been poetry, the Houston-bred poet has experienced unbridled success not only on-stage, but off-stage as an author. She is also CEO of her publishing company, "Onney Publishing & Performances, Inc.", which has become a lauded template and formula for upstart and thriving authors looking for success. Onney published her first book "Infinite Silhouettes" in 2007. She then went on to publish "Cycle of Alteration" by Ablyss Gillespie, "Old Skool's Sex Tools" (Volumes I, II & III) by Howard McAfee, "In Its Entirety" by Aja Fitzgerald, and "Praying for a Better Day" by Marquis Jonkins to name a few. Onney perfected her craft in journalism and editing as the Entertainment Editor and columnist for the

"Houston Sun Newspaper" from the years of 2008-2011.

The talented thespian is equally praised for her work on the screen and stage as an actor, songwriter, singer and model. Onney has performed at venues across the country, opening for Ron Isley, Angela Winbush, BET Comedians Shawn Harris, Shang & Michael Blackston, along with actor and author Darrin Henson, and many more. She is featured on Houston rapper & radio personality Kiotti's CD, entitled "Almost Famous", as well as Houston rapper Mankyne's mix tape released in 2014, entitled "Serve-All Mix Tape".

As a feature artist and actress, Onney appears in 'Rent-A-Car', executively produced by Frank White, where she performs her hit single, *"October"*. She also featured in "A Gangland's Love Story", executively produced by Greg Carter, where she performs *"Mr. Incredible"*. She received writer's credit in "A Gangland's Love Story" for writing the poems recited in the movie by Reagan Gomez, A.J. Lamas and herself. Two songs from her album, "BeYou2Feel Music" were also selected for the movie's soundtrack. Both films were picked up by Maverick (owned by Madonna) and can be found in your local Redbox.

Onney landed her first major role in a stage play when she auditioned for Submission Adultery Disease (S.A.D.), a play written and directed by Ablyss Gillespie. This play was held in the historical Silver House Theatre located in Houston, Texas. Acting opened Onney up to a whole new avenue of expression. She has also shared the stage with The Legendary Shirley Murdock while maintaining the lead female role in the gospel stage play tour

"Heaven Ain't Hard to Find," directed by Curtis Von, the lead male role, and produced by 3Wise Men Productions.

After taking a brief hiatus, in 2012, Onney performed at the Def Poetry Jam Summit put on by Co-Founder Danny Simmons in front of a crowd of 5,000+ at the Miller Outdoor Theatre in Houston, Texas. She was then cast for the stage play and movie "Lyfe's Poetic Revenge", a play written and directed by Rae-Shell D. Fletcher, where she played the double role of Bridgett and also herself. The play was held at the Country Playhouse Theatre in Houston. Soon thereafter, Onney landed another major role in a stage play when she featured in "*Bougie,* Broke & Single" a play written and directed by Ablyss Gillespie and held at the Hobby Center in Houston.

In 2013, Onney received the "Woman of the Year Award" presented by the Houston Sun Newspaper and the City of Houston. The guest speakers on her behalf consisted of Congresswoman Sheila Jackson Lee, Mayor Annise Parker, Congressman Al Green and many more. She was honored for her community participation in Adopt-A-Diva Camps, a program that mentors young girls from the ages of 12-18, as well as her contributions annually in Juneteenth Celebrations at the historical Emancipation Park located in 3rd Ward Houston.

Although Onney's resume seems substantial, her accomplishments did not come easily. Coming from a lineage of talent was great, but Onney chose not to use her roots as a pass to open doors, thus changing her name from Lanora Laws to Onney (Meaning: *To desire to be great*). Onney born Lanora Laws, now Lanora Jackson, was born and raised in

Houston, Texas. Onney became a mother to her first son at the young age of 16. Even with the challenge of being a teen mother, Onney graduated from Willowridge High School at 16 and went on to become MS Certified and receive her Bachelor's in Business Administration with a Minor in Accounting from the University of Honolulu on a scholarship.

Onney is the proud mother of 3 sons, now ages 20, 17, and 12; the majority of their years were spent being raised by her alone. Onney has overcome many trials and set-backs in her life from becoming a teen mother, to experiencing divorce, and even becoming temporarily paralyzed, but she refused to let anything sway her from her goals.

Most recently, Onney and Ablyss decided to create Selfish Subjects Inc., a joint venture in which they bring their creative talents together to educate the world on social issues as well as provide entertainment. Coincidentally, Onney & Ablyss attended the same high school and lived one block away from one another while growing up. Yet they did not cross paths until they joined the creative world of the poetry scene in Houston. After working together on multiple projects, these ladies couldn't deny the creative chemistry and desire they both shared for the arts. It only made sense to join forces in creating great reads for years to come.

Onney recently remarried and resides in Pearland, Texas, with her husband and children. With both she and her husband having children from previous marriages, creating a blended family has helped her to gain a whole new understanding on how co-parenting from different households can be an extensive challenge to all involved. Who better

to author a book of this nature than someone that
has experience from every angle?

TABLE OF CONTENTS

self·ish
selfiSH/
adjective
adjective: **selfish**

1. (of a person, action, or motive) lacking consideration for others; concerned chiefly with one's own personal profit or pleasure.

"I joined them for selfish reasons"

synonyms: egocentric, egotistic, egotistical, egomaniacal, self-centered, self-absorbed, self-obsessed, self-seeking, self-serving, wrapped up in oneself; inconsiderate, thoughtless, unthinking, uncaring, uncharitable; mean, miserly, grasping, greedy, mercenary, acquisitive, opportunistic; *informal* looking after number one

"he is just selfish by nature"

antonyms: altruistic

1: concerned excessively or exclusively with oneself: seeking or concentrating on one's own advantage, pleasure, or well-being without regard for others

2: arising from concern with one's own welfare or advantage in disregard of others <a *selfish* act>

1

Why Bash?

It ain't mine...

I never slept with her...

She just trying to trap me...

Don't call her until we know IT's ours...

Let's just wait for these test results...

She so low class...

She wish I was her baby daddy...

Blah Blah Blah Blah...

In the case of ....You are the father!!!

100% NOBODY ELSE!!!!

You Wanted It, You Take Care of It

"You wanted it, you take care of it." Too often, these words have been said to many single mothers around the globe. In many cases, it's due to an unplanned pregnancy that the mother chose not to terminate. Seemingly so, these mothers are left to bear the burden of becoming single parents simply because they chose to preserve the innocent lives growing in their wombs. Why does this happen so frequently in our society? Is this fair?

Here we have Jayson. Jayson is in his early 20's attending college on a fully paid football scholarship. He is young, good-looking, and by the looks of his GPA, his future seems to be quite promising. He's been with his on-again-off-again girlfriend since he was a sophomore in high school. Unfortunately, now that they are attending two different schools, they are only able to spend time during the holidays and summer breaks. Things seemed to be going smoothly until...

Text (Stacy): *Hey Jayson. Call me back as soon as you get this message. I really need to speak to you its urgent!*

Text (Jayson): *What's up? I am headed to football practice with the fellas and it's too loud in here. Can you text it?*

Text (Stacy): *No babe, I really would rather you call.*

What could be so important? Jayson thought to himself.

"I bet she just wants to complain about something she saw on social media again. I'll call her after practice," he said under his breath, as he walked into the locker room with the rest of the team.

Exhausted from practice and a long day of classes, Jayson forgot to call his girlfriend back.

Knock! Knock! Knock!!!!

As Jayson rushed to the door with sleep in his eyes, he was greeted by a young, distraught girlfriend with a face full of tears...

"Why didn't you call me back last night? Why have you been avoiding me? Are you cheating on me?" Stacy asked question after question while pushing her way through the door without waiting on a response for the previous question.

Jayson just stood there, confused about the surprise visit to his dorm. He stopped her and asked, "You drove all the way here just to ask me why I didn't call you back?"

Stacy looked down before responding and then looked him straight in his eyes and mumbled, "I'm pregnant."

"How did you let this happen? I thought you were on the pill?!" yelled Jayson, "I can't have any kids right now! I have my whole future in front of me. How far along are you?"

4

"I am 12 weeks, and what you mean how did I let this happen?! It takes two remember?" Stacy replied as she wiped the tears from her cheeks.

"Well you can't keep it. I don't want any kids right now. So when are we going to take care of this?" he asked without considering how she might feel about it. Stacy told Jayson that she was not having an abortion as it went against her moral beliefs.

Hoping that he would change his mind with time, Stacy left his dorm. She wasn't ready for a child either. Her whole life was in front of her as well... What will she do now that she's having a baby? Questions were spinning in her head during her four hour ride back to her own college campus...

Several months later, Stacy had a three month-old baby. Since she was now a single mother, she had to drop out of college to work and support her beautiful baby girl. Times had been extremely hard for her; money had been very tight with all of the new responsibilities that came with being a full-time single parent.

Without any other option, Stacy reached out to Jayson, who had not been very present since the mention of the pregnancy.

"Yo!" Jayson answered the phone, clueless to who was on the other end of the phone line.

"Hi Jayson, it's me, Stacy," she replied.

"What's up?" he asked, with a tone of annoyance upon hearing her voice.

"Well, I am in a bit of a bind. I just spent all that I had left on childcare for Navaeh and she's out of formula. I was hoping that you could send me some money to help out."

"Naw, I don't have it, I told you that I didn't want any kids! You wanted it, you take care of it!!!" he said before pressing the end button on his cell phone...How Selfish...

Bottom of the Steps

Something about the bottom steps where a child has to wait for a father to arrive.

BD: I will come and pick you up around 4:00p.m.

Child: Okay Daddy, see you then.

(Mama is sitting on the couch shaking her head because Baby Daddy is never on time and barely shows up.)

BM: I don't think he is coming. It's now 9:00p.m., and he should have been here hours ago, sweetie. Go and put your clothes on for bed. Hopefully, he will call before you go to bed.

Child: I know my daddy loves me, and he is coming. I can feel it.

BM: Ok baby, well Mama is going to bed, but if the doorbell rings or he knocks, come and get me before you leave so I can give you a kiss and lock up.

10:00pm, 11:00p.m., 12:00a.m., 1:00am..........6:00a.m.

Mama wakes up to find her child at the bottom of the stairs, knocked out. Then the phone rings.

BM: Hello?

BD: Sorry, my girlfriend planned a romantic dinner for me, and I totally forgot about it, but I am on my way to pick him up right now.

BM: Ok.

BD: See you in a little bit.

Child: Was that my daddy?

BM: Yes, he is on his way.

Child: Why is he just now calling me?

BM: You will have to ask him when he gets here.

How Selfish...

Tax Time... Can I get a Kickback?

"*It's Tax Time, so can I get a kickback?*" How many of us have been asked this question? Here's the scenario, we have a mother, father, and son involved. The father has only spent time with his son 28 days out of the previous year, yet when the mother (who has custody of the child) files for her tax return, he has the nerve to ask her to split it 50/50. He has been paying $200 a month in Child Support and feels entitled to a kickback. The mother has been spending $75 weekly in childcare, roughly $300 a month.

Of course we know that the expenses do not stop at child care; a child needs food, shelter, clothing, and medical care along with anything else that may arise.

Needless to say, this mother felt that splitting her tax return with the absentee father would be unacceptable. So this father did the unthinkable!! When this mother decided to file her taxes, her hopes for relief through a tax return were quickly crushed. You guessed it!! He filed his taxes first and claimed this child as a dependent without giving the mother notice or a dime!! Therefore, the $3600 child care expense credit went out of the window, along with any other tax refunds she would have received.

How Selfish...

*

***

I should be able to see my child whenever I want!

***

*

Not at This Hour

"Jordan, let mommy tuck you in now, it's bedtime!" said Tabitha with a cheerful tone, as she made her way up the stairs towards Jordan's room. It had been a long day, full of visits from friends and family, and it seemed that all Tabitha could think of was having some quiet time. Tabitha had it all planned out. She was going to catch up on her pre-recorded shows that she had missed earlier that evening, then take a warm bubble bath. Maybe even have a glass of wine or two while she read one of those Vicky Stringer books that she seemed to never have time to read with her hectic schedule.

2 Hours Later... Approximately 11:00 p.m...

"Whewww," sighed Tabitha, as she flopped on the couch with a book in hand. The house was so quiet you could hear the clock ticking on the mantle over the fireplace. It was just what Tabitha needed. It wasn't long before she was out... So much for catching up on her good read. Moments later, her sleep was broken when she heard the doorbell ring. Startled by the sound of the bell, she sat straight up on the couch and glanced over at the clock.

As she wiped the sleep from her eyes, the bell rang again, and it was followed by several knocks on the door. She approached the door with caution and quietness so she could get a peek through the peep-hole to see who could possibly be ringing her doorbell at that hour.

When she looked through the peep hole she immediately recognized the person ringing her doorbell. It was Sebastian, her son's father. Before opening the door, she glanced at the clock once more, and it read 12:03 AM. This was not a common thing between the two of them, so she just knew that something had to be wrong. Why else would Sebastian be ringing her doorbell at this hour?

The relationship between the two of them was pretty cordial; no history of disputes or anything of that nature, so she wasn't worried about her safety at all. As her mind filled with thoughts of what could possibly have him standing on the other side of her door, she opened the door with a puzzled look on her face.

"What's wrong?" Tabitha asked before he could get a word out.

"Nothing Tab. I was in the area, so I wanted to drop in and check on my little man. How is he doing anyway?" Sebastian said calmly, as if it was 2:00 P.M. in the afternoon.

"He's fine, he's asleep and it's after midnight!" Tabitha said with an attitude, as she crossed her arms to let Sabastian know that she was obviously not appreciative of the hour that he chose to visit.

"Aww you tripping, it's not like he has school in the morning, and you're off on Sundays. You must have company or something," Sebastian replied in a sarcastic manner.

"What does any of that have to do with you coming here at midnight? Don't you think it's rather disrespectful of my personal space to just pop-up at my home at this hour?" Tabitha asked before pausing to give him a moment to answer. Sebastian just stood there with a confused look on his face, as if Tabitha was speaking an unfamiliar language to him.

Without giving an answer to her questions, he asked with a tone of aggressiveness, "So are you going to let me see my son or not?"

Tabitha had never been in this position before, but she knew she didn't want to start any new habits that could potentially cause problems later. Even though she was single, she still wanted healthy boundaries established from the beginning. So when she did find Mr. Right, her baby daddy wouldn't kill her vibe by ringing her doorbell at all times of the night just because he's in the area.

"No Sebastian, not now. It's too late, and he's asleep anyway," she replied.

"It's too late? What do you mean it's too late? I can come and see my son whenever I want to. He's my son!!" Sebastian yelled before Tabitha could give him another reason why he couldn't see Jordan.

"Indeed he is, but this is my house and I would appreciate it if the next time you decide you want to see your son that you choose a better hour to show up and please make sure you call before you come. Let this be the last time that you ring my doorbell at this hour on a non-emergency. Goodnight," Tabitha replied as she started to close the door.

"Oh, it's like that?" he asked as if that was supposed to change Tabitha's mind.

"It is" were the last words she said as she closed the door.

Weekend Visitation

(Weekend visitation: Friday 6:00p.m.-Sunday 6:00p.m.)

BD: Hey I need to drop the little one off at 2:00p.m. Sunday. Is this okay?

You, as the father, only pick the child up every other weekend, so in the mind of a Baby Mama:

You only come twice each month...

You don't call to check on the child during the week...

You don't assist during the week...

I have the child nearly the entire month, and I may have plans for the entire time you limit yourself to...

What if I planned to go out of town and my flight doesn't come in till 4:00p.m.?

*

***

Why is it that I have to pay child support but I am not allowed to request receipts for what she is spending the money on?

***

*

Signed Sealed & Delivered

*Th*ings finally seemed to be taking a turn for the better in Brandon's life. He had just gotten off of parole and was finally getting caught up on two of his child support cases. Unfortunately for him, he still had two other cases hanging over his shoulders. It was not the life that Brandon had planned for himself, but it seemed that he always got caught up in situations with women that he had no intentions on actually settling down with. He had just been sowing his oats and living life at the time. Now that he was actually working on being a better man, the first thing he wanted to secure was financial stability.

Perhaps the child support payments wouldn't have been so much of an issue if he didn't have four baby mamas. When you have multiple cases, the Attorney General's Office treats every case separately if the children have different mothers. It seemed that no one knew that struggle better than Brandon. Four baby mamas all with their hands out, left Brandon in a complicated financial mess.

Whenever Brandon tried to go to the Attorney General's office to get his payments lowered in order for him to be able to make ends meet, they would redirect him, telling him to get an attorney. With more than half of his net income going to child support and the other half going strictly to rent, bills and surviving until the next check, there was no way Brandon could afford to pay for a lawyer.

17

At that moment, Brandon determined that the Attorney General's Office wasn't on the father's side. Without any regard to whether his feelings were right or wrong, Brandon felt that child support was just a system that the mothers used as a form of control.

Brandon had built great relationships with all but one of his children: his oldest daughter, Myah. When Myah was conceived, Brandon had no idea that her mother was even pregnant until after her birth. Brandon encountered her mother Sabrina one night after the club and a few hours later, they were pulling into the Motel 6 off the Interstate. Brandon didn't think anything of it. He was high on life. He had just finished an 8 year bid in state prison. He was free after being wrongfully convicted of a crime when he was 18 years old. He finally had a chance to enjoy his youth. He had just turned 27. He was handsome and smart. He was very educated since he used his time in prison to achieve two degrees and develop a trade. So again, the world was his oyster.

After Brandon's encounter with Sabrina that night, they talked on the phone frequently and texted one another throughout the day for the following three weeks. They met up for drinks one time after that, but something had changed because after they saw one another in person the second time, Brandon stopped answering her calls and her texts. In fact, he blocked her! Brandon took one look at Sabrina and said to himself, "Man! I must have been tripping with myself that night, or those drinks must have been really good. This chic looks like a bear-gorilla! I mean, she *fine*, but damn."

18 months later...

One Sunday afternoon, while Brandon was at the local car wash waiting on his car to finish being serviced, in walked Sabrina. She had lost a little weight, and her skin had cleared up beautifully. In fact, she was actually quite tolerable. Maybe the last time they saw one another, she was having an *off* day. Either way, she still was brick house fine.

As Sabrina walked in, she immediately locked eyes with Brandon. She had a look on her face as if she had seen a ghost. Unbeknownst to Brandon, Sabrina had made great efforts to find him. She had even started to frequent the club Mel's, where she originally met him, hoping to potentially bump into him again. She recalled the numerous calls and texts that she had sent to the number he gave her without a reply.

It seemed that everything came rushing to Sabrina's mind all at once. Brandon had robbed her of the opportunity to tell him that he was the father of their 10 month old daughter. This was Sabrina's chance, and she didn't want to blow it. Sabrina maintained her composure as Brandon walked in her direction.

"Hello stranger, long time no see," Brandon said to Sabrina as he approached her, giving her a full-body inspection with only his eyes. He couldn't help but notice her well-manicured hands and feet that went so well with her stone-washed denim jeans and Jimmy Choo shoes. She wasn't *all that* in the face, but her swag was on a thousand, to say the least. This was a complete turn on for Brandon, and with his good looks and charm, he figured that once again, Sabrina was going to be easy bait.

Brandon stood 6'2" with a caramel complexion. He had dimples that you could lose yourself in, and a smile that would turn the hardest woman soft. His hair had enough waves to make you sea-sick, and based on his build, he never missed a gym appointment.

"Wow! Looky what we have here!" Sabrina said as she masked all of her emotions with a coy smile. A conversation ensued and before long, Brandon and Sabrina had exchanged numbers again. Even though Sabrina had practiced over a thousand times what she'd say to Brandon if she ever saw him again, she couldn't bring herself to utter a word about Myah. Sabrina didn't want to run him off before he even had the opportunity to see the beautiful daughter they had created.

"Ma'am, your car is ready!" a young gentleman said as he peeked through the door to get Sabrina's attention. Both Brandon and Sabrina turned to walk towards Sabrina's car.

"Is that you?" Brandon asked as the young gentleman held open the door to a white 2007 Mercedes Benz S550.

"That's me! Be sure to call me so we can link up," Sabrina said as she sashayed her way into the car.

"Lil' Mama must be doing something right," Brandon thought to himself. He was determined to link up with Sabrina after this brief encounter.

Several weeks later, the time finally came. Brandon had been so persistent about seeing Sabrina again that he invited her over to his place.

Little did he know, this was perfect for her. Now, she'd know exactly where to find him if she needed him. It wasn't long before Brandon decided to shoot his shot to bed her again. At that moment, Sabrina felt like it was time to reveal a secret that she had been holding onto for far too long. Before leaving Brandon's home that evening, Sabrina suggested that he come over the next day to visit. She sweetened the deal by adding, "I'll prepare lunch and you can check out my new condo."

"Bet!" Brandon replied, accepting her invitation.

The next day...

Ding-Dong! The doorbell sounded off over the soft music playing in the background.

"That must be your daddy," Sabrina said under her breath as she placed Myah in her high-chair before making her way to the door.

"This is some place you have here!" Brandon uttered in admiration of her condo and décor as he followed Sabrina into the kitchen.

"Thanks hun, I do what I can. Would you like a glass of wine?" she said, responding to his compliment. Before Brandon could answer, he was startled by the surprise guest sitting in the high-chair.

"Well, who is this adorable little angel?" he asked, ill prepared for what was to follow.

"Funny you asked, because I've been meaning to talk to you about just that. Brandon, this is Myah.

She just made 11 months old. She's my daughter...
our daughter," Sabrina said, looking Brandon
directly in his eyes. Brandon immediately started
calculating time in his head and said to himself, *Well,
I be damned. She does have my eyes and dimples.
Could this be? I wasn't trying to sign up for all that.*

Not knowing exactly how to respond to this,
the first thing that left Brandon's lips was, "How do
you know for sure?"

Sabrina didn't take offense to the question
considering Myah was the result of a one-night-
stand. When they met, Sabrina was in a dry-spell,
and it had been months since she had sex with
anyone else prior to sleeping with Brandon. She
knew that would be hard for anyone in Brandon's
position to believe.

"Prior to sleeping with you, I hadn't slept
with anyone else in months. I was totally
rebounding from my ex when I met you. By the time
I found out I was pregnant and tried to contact you,
you never answered my calls or returned my texts. I
tried looking for you, but honestly, I didn't know
where to start. I didn't even know your last name
until recently. I couldn't even give her your last
name if I wanted to. So embarrassing..." she said
with a tone of disgust. "If it makes you feel better, we
can take a DNA test," she added.

Deep down inside Brandon knew Myah was
his child, but still, he wanted to be sure, so he
agreed, and the appointment was made.

"Let's hear it doc," Brandon said at their
appointment to hear the results.

"Well Mr. Daniels, it looks like you have a daughter. The results indicate that you are 99.999% Myah's father."

Brandon sat there stunned at the information provided by the doctor sitting in front of him. He never intended on becoming a father this way, but it was his reality.

The first year after discovering he had a daughter was touch-and-go. Brandon had no genuine interest in Sabrina and the fact that they shared a child together was merely circumstantial. It wasn't long before their communication with one another dwindled into a non-existent conversation.

Before he knew it, Brandon was being served to show up for court for a child support hearing. Brandon felt like he didn't want any of those problems, so again, he went off the radar. He moved when his lease was up and changed his number. He didn't have time for any of that and surely wasn't trying to give Sabrina a dime. He had no problem buying what his daughter needed, but the thought of having to pay her out of every check was enough to make him quit his salaried job and work contract to keep from having his checks garnished. Besides, from the looks of things, Sabrina was doing fine without him having to give her anything. She drove a Mercedes Benz, lived in an expensive high-rise condo and her wardrobe consisted of all things high-end, so what could she possibly need with *his* money, he thought.

After a few years of Brandon ducking the court system, the Attorney General along with his past decisions had finally caught up with him. He hadn't spoken to Sabrina since Myah was 2 years old

23

and Myah was now 7. Getting out of this jam was going to be even more difficult than he assumed since Sabrina had gotten married. Brandon knew he couldn't get her to be lenient and wave some of that arrearage by using his undeniable charm. He had more than $43,000 in back child support and interest, and if he didn't come up with something quick, jail time was definitely on the horizon.

Undecided about what to do, Brandon took a chance by reaching out to Sabrina in hopes of getting her to understand his current situation. Perhaps she'd be willing to agree to waive at least half of that amount. Sabrina thought long and hard on the decision before bringing it to Todd, her current husband, who had been actively raising Myah as his own since Myah was three years old.

Todd had asked Sabrina before to allow Myah to carry his last name so that they all could share the same name. The way he looked at things, Myah was *his* daughter and he didn't really see Sabrina's point in even asking Brandon to be a part of Myah's life anymore, child support included.

Todd suggested that Sabrina ask Brandon to forfeit his parental rights by signing them over to him since *he* was the father in Myah's life. He told Sabrina to use this as an option for waiving the back child support, and this is exactly what she did.

When Sabrina initially made the suggestion to Brandon, it infuriated him. He couldn't believe that she would have the audacity to even make that suggestion. What type of father would he be to do something like this? He pondered on the topic for over a week before making his decision.

Brandon weighed it out in his mind in every way you could think of. He finally decided that regardless of what that piece of paper said, it wasn't going to change the fact that Myah was *his* daughter. He promised himself that once he became financially secure again, that he would reach out to his daughter and try to explain to her why he came to his decision. Having the weight of this child support case off of his back would leave him to only worry about paying the arrears on one case instead of the two he had lingering over his head. The more and more he thought about those Ramen Noodle diets that he had become accustomed to, the more enticing the suggestion became.

Needless to say, when the day came, Brandon signed away his parental rights to Myah, and he was delivered from the financial strain of paying that back child support. Shortly thereafter, Sabrina and Todd relocated to another state and Brandon never heard from his daughter again. Myah may never know who her *real* father is now...

*

***

Why do I have to pay 50% on medical expenses when I have to pay for health insurance monthly?

***

*

Medical Fees

BM: My out-of-pocket expenses for these medical bills have been paid, now I need your half.

BD: I'm not giving you any money; I'll take it to the child support office.

BM: That's for child support, and it won't go towards the medical expenses.

BD: Stop trying to take advantage of me. I am not giving you any money outside of what is required through the child support office.

BM: What? *(hangs up phone)*

The baby mama is left with no choice but to turn in the paperwork on medical expenses owed. When she does this, the child support office sends him a letter to request the 50% owed to his baby mama or a court date would be set up.

Later at the Attorney General's Office...

BD: I don't understand why I am here because I sent in the $450.00 to the books for child support. It should all go together.

Child Support Office: Sir, child support is for child support. We do not have an account set up to separate child support from medical expenses because medical expenses that you owe the custodial parent are paid directly to the custodial parent. If you refuse to give her the check, then a court date will be set up. You will be forced to pay your half of the medical expenses, Attorney General's legal fees, as well as your own. It's best and cheaper to pay the medical expenses directly to her in order to avoid all those extra fees. And in the future, if this happens again, try to pay your portion directly to the medical facility if you don't feel comfortable giving her the cash. Either way, you are responsible for 50% of all medical bills incurred after the insurance pays their portion.

Looks like BM tried to tell him, but he had to hear it for himself...

The Insurance Card Saga

In most cases, the non-custodial parent that pays child support is responsible for providing health insurance.

As a baby mama, you come across those baby daddies who don't want to provide health insurance, and if they do provide insurance for their child, they refuse to give you the insurance card. Some baby daddies want you to call them each time you go to the doctor, and the card can be used then. But in a case of a real emergency, this can be a huge inconvenience and can potentially prohibit you from getting the necessary care needed to treat your child.

When you have a child with someone and your relationship doesn't work out, it can be stressful. My baby daddy was unhappy when he wasn't allowed to control certain things, so he tried his best to control things that he felt were in his control. He was responsible for providing health insurance for our little one. He felt I should contact him every time she became sick and then he'd meet me there to use the card. I felt that was a bit excessive, being that he worked on the other side of town. We didn't really get along or converse in a mature manner. I decided I was tired of having to fight with him at the attorney general's office.

The only way I knew I could get the insurance card was to go to the hospital when the little one was sick. When the bill would arrive, I would just take the bill down to the attorney general's office to request 50% reimbursement. Instead of following the rules and reimbursing me, he would place the money on the books for child support payment. When he did this, the attorney general's office informed him that medical expenses are to be paid directly to the custodial parent. His money was lost, and from this, I received the insurance card and the medical expenses reimbursement.

Baby mamas, how do you get around this? The child support office (in some states) says each person has to provide 50% of medical expenses. Every time your child gets sick, take them to the emergency room. Report the total to the child support office, and let them set up a court date to receive 50%. I bet you will receive an insurance card then. It isn't to be spiteful, but this may allow them to see the inconvenience that comes with being selfishly petty.

Misplaced Concern

BM: Junior is not feeling well. I'm headed to the hospital with him.

BD: Ok, let me know how it goes.

BM: Will you meet me there?

BD: The game is on. Just call me and let me know what the doctor says when you leave.

A few weeks later...

BD: I need to bring Junior home early.

BM: Why?

BD: My ex-girlfriend's sister is in the hospital and I need to get up there.

BM: Really?

Never Available

He was only 7 years old, and he couldn't understand why all of his friends had fathers, and he didn't. Of course he knew he had a father, but why didn't his father come to see him?

He was at the age where he could call and invite his dad to all of the events that he wanted his dad to attend. Even with the invites, his dad always seemed to have something else to do or would promise to come and never show up.

Why doesn't my father come to my Little League games? Am I not good enough? Does my dad hate me? What is wrong with me?

Those are the thoughts that consumed his young mind...

Married No Kids...

BM: I have good news.

BD: What?

BM: We're pregnant.

BD: Damn really?

BM: Yes. You don't seem excited.

BD: I'm not because this is not in my plans.

BM: What you mean?

BD: I'm not ready.

BM: Well it's a bit late for that. Looks like you have some preparing to do.

BD: You're not considering keeping it, are you?

Girlfriend Saga

As a baby mama, the radars are up and the crazy sensitive level of being a mother, (especially a first time mother) is scary.

The doorbell rings. A random woman is at the door.

Girlfriend: My name is Jayla and I'm Eric's girlfriend. He wants me to pick up Erica for his weekend.

BM: (*Calls baby daddy in front of her*) Who is Jayla and why would you send her to pick up Erica and not discuss it with me first?

BD: The paperwork from the Attorney General's Office states that I can send who I want for my pick-up and drop-off, and there is nothing you can do about it.

BM: That is all well and good, but you are sending a person to my home that I have never seen, and you expect for me to just give her our child? That is truly crazy.

BD: No, because I am a responsible adult and I would not send someone who is not competent or isn't a good person to pick up my child.

He's missing the whole point...Where is the respect?

Not Out of My Check

$\mathcal{H}$e decided that he didn't want the Attorney General taking money out of his check to send to his children's mother. He couldn't stand her. So he quit his job and started working contract so he'd get paid under the table.

Now he could send money how and when he wanted to, which wasn't very often. As a result, his children are suffering because he is too selfish to see that it isn't about *him*, but about the well-being of his children...

How Selfish...

96-Hour Father

What is a 96-Hour father?

24 hours in a day

168 hours in a week

672 hours in a month (depending on the month)

672

-96 (Every other weekend visits with Father
excluding 5th Friday's)

=576 (Hours Mom has Child/Children in 4 weeks)

These numbers are based on the premise that you
are a father who, at the very least, has your children
every other weekend. Some fathers go months
without seeing their children.

But baby daddies complain about paying child
support...

I'm Not a Baby-sitter

*H*ere we have Trese, age 20, her 2 children ages 4 and 1 (boys), and her husband Aaron, age 24. Aaron is in the Navy, and they have been stationed to the 22nd Street Naval Station in San Diego, California. Their location was unfamiliar grounds for the young mother. No family or friends anywhere in sight. Considering that Trese was from Dallas, Texas, her southern accent and demeanor made it obvious that she wasn't from around there.

Aaron had been stationed there for some time, but when the military housing became available, Trese and the kids came to join him. After a year of being there together, they had settled into a routine. While Trese spent the majority of her time working and taking care of the kids, Aaron's hanging out with the guys after work had become the norm.

Trese had made it obvious that she wanted a break from the kids for a night to go out on the town, and Aaron had the perfect idea in mind. Aaron invited her to a gathering that most of his other friends would be bringing their wives or girlfriends to. Trese attended, excited to feel youthful again. There she met a young girl her age from New Orleans, Louisiana. Sharon was her name. She too had two young boys that happened to be the same ages as Trese's boys. Combining their similarities along with the southern demeanor they both possessed, they hit it off. Best friends they became.

Trese and Sharon were able to include their kids on their outings, although most of them consisted of Chuck-E-Cheese, the zoo, or the park. After months of consistently having the kids on every outing, they both decided that they should go out for Trese's 21st Birthday.

Sharon called her husband on his cell to see if he wouldn't mind planning to stay in with their kids Friday night, and he had no problem. That was easy, Trese thought, but Trese wasn't sure it would go so well for her. Trese went home and awaited Aaron's arrival. That evening during conversation, she asked him if he could plan to be home because she wanted to go and hang out with Sharon on Friday in celebration of her birthday the next day. He agreed and assured her he didn't mind her going at all. Trese was so excited. Although she kept calm, she could barely contain herself. The planning had begun... a girl's night out.

The next few days to follow consisted of shopping and preparing for the big celebration. Trese had never been out in San Diego, and she was finally getting that much-needed break from the everyday hustle and bustle of working and kids.

Friday arrived, and Trese was ready for her evening out. She finished her work day and was off to pick up the boys from daycare. On her way home, she called Aaron to see if he had already left the Naval Base. To her surprise, she was told that he had taken the day off. Aaron was never a real romantic when it came to surprises, but Trese couldn't help but suspect Aaron had some sort of birthday surprise for her.

When Trese arrived home, Aaron wasn't anywhere to be found, but she couldn't spend time trying to figure out where he was. She had an exciting evening planned, and she wanted to be ready when Sharon arrived. As she completed her finishing touches on her hair, her telephone rang; it was Sharon alerting her that she would be there in ten minutes. The kids were already bathed, fed, and put to bed. But, where was Aaron? Trese was so busy trying to be ready when Sharon arrived, that she didn't think to call Aaron again. After calling him several times with her calls going straight to voicemail, she began to get upset.

"I know he remembers that he said that he would be here," Trese said under her breath.

Sharon arrived and Trese invited her in to wait on Aaron since they couldn't leave until he arrived. An hour later, Aaron walked through the front door, as if nothing was wrong. He walked right past Sharon and Trese, grabbed a duffel bag from the bedroom, and headed to the front door.

Trese stopped him to remind him of their arrangement with the kids for the evening. Aaron reached for the doorknob, looked back sharply at Trese, and said, "I am not a baby-sitter."

Before Trese could utter a word, the door had already closed behind him. Her plans for a night of fun and birthday celebrations were over just like that...

How Selfish?

Real Men Don't Babysit Their Kids, They Raise Them...

Words Do Hurt

$\mathcal{D}$avid, age 37, had been raising his daughter Gabriel from the time she was 1-year-old, only receiving help from his sister and his mother. At thirteen, Gabby's mind was very impressionable entering her teenage years. In junior high, she struggled at times to fit in because most of her friends had something at home that she didn't, *a mom.*

Gabby was placed in her father's custody when she was taken away from her mother by CPS for prostitution and drug abuse. Gabby had always believed that her mother was suffering from an illness, and that is why her father had to raise her. This was what she had always been told by her grandmother and her aunt. When Gabby was three years old, David relocated from Atlanta to Houston so that he could be closer to his family and have some assistance with raising Gabby.

With David relocating to another city and state, this made it almost impossible for Celeste, Gabby's mother, to see her. Due to the fact that Celeste was in and out of rehabilitation facilities, David felt that it was best to keep Gabby away from Celeste. David didn't want Gabby getting hurt or seeing her mother in that way, and it seemed that Celeste just couldn't stay clean. She would do well for a few months, and then it was either back to the same drugs or a different drug of choice. This is not the example that David wanted for Gabby.

When Gabby began to go through puberty and develop as a young teen, she longed for the mother-daughter relationship that all of her friends had with their mothers. With all of those feelings and emotions surfacing, Gabby became more and more inquisitive about her mother and her mother's whereabouts.

David eventually became annoyed with all of the questions that Gabby had about her mother. In fact, he began to resent it. David lost two jobs because he took off work with Gabby while she was sick. The first time, when she was five, she contracted chicken pox from another child at preschool. The second time, when she was nine, she had influenza that lasted almost two weeks. David knew first-hand the sacrifices that single mothers always seemed to talk about. He felt like single fathers didn't get enough recognition, and single mothers seemed to get all the sympathy in the world that fathers rarely received.

Mother's Day approached, and for Gabby's art class, the assignment was Mother's Day cards. When Gabby returned home from school that day, she couldn't wait to show her dad the beautiful card she had designed for her mother. Gabby thought for sure this would make her sick mother feel better, wherever she was. So, with hopes of being able to send her mother her custom Mother's Day card, Gabby began what had become routine...asking questions. David didn't really know how to handle all of the questions and knew that he would have to come up with something to get Gabby's mind off the topic of Celeste.

The home phone rang as Gabby was waiting on an answer from David.

"Saved by the bell," David thought to himself. This gave David the perfect opportunity to change the subject without much effort.

"Gabby, excuse me for a moment while I take this call. It's Granny," David said to Gabby in a way to let her know to leave the room.

On her way to her bedroom, she couldn't help but hear her father say, "No, Gabby was just in here asking me about Celeste."

Hearing her mother's name stopped her right in her tracks. It was like a cement brick was placed at her feet. She knew that she would get in trouble if her dad caught her listening to his conversation, but she was willing to take the chance if what he was going to say next would possibly answer some of the questions that he had obviously been avoiding.

"I don't know Mama. I wish she would just stop asking about her! Celeste is nothing but a prostitute-junkie that will never be anything. I wish she would just die already! She has caused enough grief in this family. Did you hear about her last escapade? Well, supposedly she went to jail for trying to sell sex to a police officer. I don't want Gabby having anything to do with that slut and I hate that she's my baby mama, I swear!" David ranted into the receiver of the phone. Unbeknownst to him, little Gabby was listening to every word.

As she stood still, her heart sank, and tears streamed down her face. She ran to her room, closed the door, and planted her head in the pillow with tears soaking the pillowcase. Gabby's heart was broken.

All this time she had thought that her mother wasn't around because she was sick. But to hear her dad speak so badly of her mom, made her feel as if he was saying those things about her. It seemed that almost immediately, the crisis that Gabby was having with her identity became even worse. Questions flooded her young and innocent mind. *Did my mom not love me? Is that why I live with my Dad? Is that why I never see her? Does Daddy not like me because of my mom?*

This information left Gabby feeling empty inside. She didn't know how to digest this information. Her dad spoke so badly about her mom to her grandmother that it made her embarrassed to even bring up the topic of her mother. This created an insecurity of inadequacy when she was around her peers and other family members. David's negative rants about Celeste without regard for considering how it would make Gabby feel if she heard it, caused wounds inside of Gabby's heart that will take more than *words* to heal.

My Child Doesn't Need a Daddy

Craig was a stubborn kind of man that always wanted the world to see things his way. He and Amber had ended the relationship when Lyric was just a few months old. Craig wasn't very consistent in his daughter's life since the ugly breakup. After three years, Amber met a wonderful man that accepted her and her young daughter as his own.

Things couldn't have been better in Amber and Lyric's lives. Then suddenly Craig was in his feelings and decided to complicate Amber and her new mate's relationship with drama...

"I don't want you bringing any men around my daughter!!" Craig yelled through the receiver of the phone.

"Why Craig, it isn't like you are in her life? I've been begging you to take interest in her since she was born, and now that we are happy, you want to pull the 'father card'? Bye Craig!" Amber said, before hanging up the receiver of the phone.

Unfortunately, this is the case for many single mothers. Some of these fathers refuse to step up to the plate until someone else steps in and does a better job than they are at being a father.

How selfish...

Confession: Ego Vs Love

BM: My boyfriend asked me to get married last week, and I am trying to figure out the best way to tell my baby daddy. He already feels threatened by my boyfriend because he moved in a year ago and our son is really taking to him. How should I go about having this conversation?

Therapist: Before I get to that answer, when did your child's father come to you with his concerns?

BM: Our son went to visit him for the weekend, and while he was there, his father asked him how things were going at home. He told his dad everything is fine, and he has another daddy. This completely set him off. He called me and asked me what was that about. I told him that I didn't teach him to say that, but he probably feels like he is a daddy figure because he lives with us and is there for him. He hung up the phone in my face.

Therapist: When he hung up, did you call him back?

BM: No I didn't. I decided to wait 'til he brought him home. When he pulled up and walked our son to the door, I asked my boyfriend to be there and speak with him to tell him he is not trying to take his place.

Therapist: How did that go?

BM: Things went all the way left. My son's father did not let him speak. He went completely off!! Out of respect for my son and I, my boyfriend just looked at him crazy. From this, the two have never spoken again. I don't know what to do.

Therapist: The best thing to do is be honest. Maybe you should write him a letter; which means he would have to read it through with no interruptions. I also feel your future husband should also write him a letter expressing how much his presence is relevant and needed.

My Son to Keep

I felt that my baby daddy always came down on me for not working a full time job, and that is fine, to each his own. As for me, I have raised four beautiful daughters who are all grown. I was raising our son as a single mother. Since he didn't think I was qualified financially, he took our son around other women, teaching him to fall in love with material things.

One afternoon, I decided to check the mail, and I received a letter from his lawyer requesting my appearance in court. I couldn't understand why he would take me to court for custody. When we met, he felt like I was unfit because my house wasn't up to *his* standards. Our son has a brain tumor and fell and injured himself while under my care. The injury was severe enough for him to need therapy, and I was not keeping up with his therapy like I should have, due to my own health issues. Of course, as his father, I didn't doubt his concerns, but to take me to court to receive full custody was a bit much.

As we discussed back and forth, our communication became an uphill battle. I realized at that moment, the father of my child didn't want me around full time. I kept asking myself why? As a single mother, I was never confronted with this from the fathers of my older children. This was the first time I had to fight to keep my son.

When I was asked by the courts why I felt that he didn't have any grounds for such a request, I explained that he was wrong for wanting full custody, that he only comes every other weekend, every other holiday, never comes to therapy because he works during the day and never attends school functions during the week because he works.

I was able to attend those events because I chose not to work full time so I could be there for all daily activities, including weekly therapy visits. I even informed the judge that I hadn't raised child support in three years.

Yes, he paid health insurance for him, but it was all on me to make sure he gets to the doctor when he is sick.

After weeks of this, I was relieved, the judge ruled in my favor. I am not a perfect mother, I don't abuse my children, and I would die for them. To this day, my child's father still treats me ugly and is truly rude to me in front of our son.

*

***

She should be content with the set fee for child support. Why does she feel she needs to ask for an increase all the time?

***

*

Take Me to Court Then...

BD: Hey, we need to talk about this child support.

BM: I'm listening.

BD: I don't have much to give you, but I can swing about fifty dollars each month.

BM: Daycare alone is five hundred dollars, so you are not even halfway.

BD: What do you think it should be?

BM: Three hundred and fifty dollars.

BD: Okay, well I can't do that.

BM: No problem then, we can let the child support office handle it.

BD: That's fine with me.

BM: See you tomorrow at noon.

Attorney General: $750.00 each month.

AWESOME!!!

Working Overtime

$\mathscr{S}$ometimes the boss will call you in to work some extra hours. Good baby mamas take all that is offered and given, but sometimes the assistance from baby daddy is not there for early morning school drop off.

Baby Daddy EXCUSES:

I HAVE TO WORK AND I DON'T WANT TO WAKE UP EARLY.

I CAN ONLY DO EVERY OTHER WEEKEND.

YOU CAN'T CALL YOUR MOTHER TO HELP?

I PAY YOU CHILD SUPPORT, SO WHY CAN'T YOU FIND A DAYCARE SERVICE?

I AM GOING OUT THE NIGHT BEFORE, SO I NEED TO GET MY REST FOR WORK.

THAT MEANS I WILL HAVE TO WAKE UP AN HOUR EARLY AND DRIVE ALL THE WAY TO YOUR SIDE OF TOWN? THAT'S TOO MUCH DRIVING!

IS THIS REALLY AN EMERGENCY?

How Selfish.............

The Call

BM: Hey.

BD: Hey, what's up?

BM: I'm pregnant.

BD: It ain't mine.

Not for Keeps

BM: Hey.

BD: What's up?

BM: I'm pregnant.

BD: I'm not ready to be a father, so I know you don't plan on keeping it. Right?

Double Standards

*W*hy is it that some baby daddies feel they are justified for their behavior but come down on baby mamas for theirs?

I seem to hear that some baby daddies say that some baby mamas have no respect for their children by bringing various men around. This may be true, but these same voices do the same thing. Ironically, since the child goes off with the baby daddy for the weekend, these baby mamas don't see this.

As a baby mama myself, I saw it firsthand. My friend has a beautiful daughter, and of course, he is not with his baby mama. His daughter received gifts from two different women one day apart from each other. Both of these women believe they are special, but they are equally being used for having stacks of money in their bank account.

This little girl sees this, and of course, the father doesn't think he is doing anything wrong because it's his life and his weekend. What is this teaching her about her father? What is this teaching her about men? She knows her father can entertain two women the same way and make them both feel special, but neither one of these ladies know they are being used for his selfish gain.

When he drops his daughter off at home, he continuously dogs the mother out for having a man living in the home because six months later she will have another man living there. Two wrongs don't make a right, but he is in no position to place the patent on respect.

Damn

BM: It's good to see you.

BD: Likewise.

BM: Well I have good news. We pregnant.

BD: You sure?

BM: Yes.

BD: Damn.

Hair Saga

*A*s a first time mother, the learning process is a daily activity that never seems to stop handing out lessons. Looking for products can be a little on the scary side since a child's sensitivity level could be high, and mothers tend to worry about the ingredients in most products.

When a child goes off with Daddy, why is it so hard for his family, girlfriend, and other females involved to cooperate and use the same products? Why does everything have to be a battle?

So the question many baby mamas ask:

BM: When your mother, sister, cousin, aunts and girlfriends go to the hair salon, do they walk in and let any hairstylist do their hair? I mean...do you let just anyone cut your hair? Just a question; no need to answer it!!! But, I do have a question or two that perhaps you *can* help me with. Why is her hair so tight? You didn't see those white pimples along the edges the entire weekend?

In dad's eyes, the baby mama is being petty, but the reality is, now her daughter suffers from irritation due to products that her skin is sensitive to, and pain from having rubber bands pulling out her edges. So it's not about being petty. It's about making sure that the child is not suffering in the co-parenting process.

He Goes There Early

BM: Hey.

BD: Hey Honey! How are you?

BM: I'm good. You?

BD: I'm better now that you answered.

BM: So why are you calling me?

BD: I just wanted to apologize for how I've been acting lately and the way I've been treating you.

BM: Ok! I accept and I am pregnant.

BD: From me?

BM: Yes.

BD: Well, I hope you are not like the other baby mamas in the world who are always taking men to the child support office.

Exaggerated Expense: Confession I

Therapist: The last time we spoke you expressed to me your concerns with your daughter's grandmother on her father's side. How have things been going since we last spoke?

BM: Well things are still the same. Yesterday she came and picked up Moon. When she came to the door, she asked, and I quote, "Why are you asking for money to raise Moon? You have a job." She went on to tell me mothers like myself make it hard for fathers like her son because they are doing the best that they can; since her son is paying me six hundred and fifty dollars each month, what more do I need?

Therapist: So how did you respond to her?

BM: I didn't. But in my mind, I wanted to tell her that she never made *his* father pay child support and because of that, he doesn't even know his father.

Therapist: This is a serious matter and I am happy you didn't say this. So, what part of her expression really set you off?

BM: She said her son is paying six hundred and fifty dollars and this is a total lie. He is only paying three hundred dollars per month. She and I cannot have a relationship, let alone bond because she is still breastfeeding a grown man.

Therapist: (laughs) That is one way to look at it. Well, I think you should sit her down and show her the documentation that shows the payments are only three hundred dollars each month. She can then confront her son and discuss.

*

***

I DON'T WANT TO PAY CHILD SUPPORT, SO I AM GOING TO TAKE HER TO COURT FOR FULL CUSTODY...

***

*

CPS...Wrong for That

In the State of Texas, when children are born within a marriage, there is no way to get around the child support order, as it is mandated by the state. Whomever the non-custodial parent is, mother or father, they will be ordered to pay child support, if one is given sole custodianship.

David and Carrie went thru an ugly divorce that ended in David having to pay an amount in child support that he was not comfortable with. This caused David to refrain from wanting to help in any other way. He was not going to help with the kids getting back and forth to school, attend functions that involved the kids, or even make himself available on the weekends that he was assigned visitation. David was adamant that as long as he was on child support, he was going to do the bare minimum to assist Carrie. Although Carrie needed the financial help to raise her two children, she needed the physical presence and assistance just as much. It made things quite difficult for her, needing to be everywhere at once.

Carrie was the single mother of two children ages 9 & 11. Seemingly so, Carrie had been doing a wonderful job raising her kids all on her own, but it was a challenge in more ways than one. Every time Carrie would ask David for help, he would tell her that if she wanted him to help, she needed to take him off of child support. She contemplated it a few times, but considering his track record of not being dependable, taking him off of child support was not much of an option when her income barely covered all of the bills and expenses that came with raising her children. She needed the help from him and didn't trust him to give it to her on his own, so this made things complicated; the child support that was in place caused an even bigger communication gap between the two of them. The resentment from David seemed to grow with every deduction from his check.

David knew that the only thing he could use to get back at Carrie was going to be through her children. There was nothing else that could really steal her joy. She took all of her hardships in stride and always seemed to greet people with a smile, no matter what she was dealing with on the inside. That was Carrie.

As David's resentment towards the situation grew, he started harassing Carrie to drop the child support, or he would take her to court for custody and make her pay child support instead. Carrie didn't seem to be bothered with David's threats as she knew she provided a clean and stable environment for her children. When it came to being a great mother, she was definitely on that list. Her children were her pride and joy, and she was theirs. Besides, David had yet to take an interest in his children since their divorce that occurred over a year ago.

Carrie landed a new job at a great company with great benefits and was starting to see the light at the end of the tunnel. With her recent income increase, she began to consider more and more to just go to the Attorney General's office and take him off of child support. Finally, she had gotten to the point where whether he helped her or not, her children wouldn't hurt for anything. Maybe then he would take part in assisting her with the kids after school.

She worked twelve minutes away and she had already adjusted her work schedule, allowing her to see her children off to school every morning. There wasn't anything else that her employer could do to assist her when it came to her schedule.

Besides, she wasn't the only employee that had children. It was a requirement for her to work her 40 hours. She would work all day without taking a lunch so she could leave in time to meet her kids at home once they arrived from the bus stop. There were times that they would get home before her, but never more than 15-20 minutes. This bothered her, but she had no other choice. With her immediate family living hours away, and not many friends to call on for help, she did what she had to do.

David knew Carrie's predicament, and he was well aware that Carrie got off work at the same time the kids were released from school. He began to put his plan into action with this perfect opportunity. This was just the ingredient he needed to end this child support once and for all.

David called CPS and reported Carrie for leaving under-aged children home alone. CPS launched a full investigation and made a visit out to Carrie's residence to monitor the home and verify the accusations. It was this day that Carrie's joy was stolen. When she pulled up in her driveway, she noticed a white car parked on the curb by the mailbox. As she exited her car, she noticed her children sitting in the backseat of this car instead of in the house where they should have been.

Her heart sank into the pit of her stomach as a well-dressed woman opened the driver's side door of the vehicle and approached her with documents in hand. As the woman began to speak, it seems that all she heard was, "You have been reported for multiple accusations of child abandonment, and we will have to remove the children from the home until a more extensive investigation is completed. Do you have any contact with the father? If so, the kids can go there instead of being placed in a facility."

As she was allowed to kiss her children before the car drove away, she knew who was behind all of this. Yes, her children were underage as thirteen is the legal 'latch-key' age to be left home alone. David was just being vindictive because he knew that she would be home fifteen minutes after they were released from the bus stop. The sad part was that he picked the kids up and dropped them off at his mother's house. He didn't even really want custody; he just wanted to be off of child support.

How Selfish...

The Nerve of Him

BD: Hey babe! I know I've been wrong and cheating on you, but I want you to know that I got a call today, and the chick says she's pregnant.

(Girlfriend looks puzzled)

BD: But I assure you, it ain't mine because we used a condom. She is just jealous of you.

Cheaper to Keep Her

BM: I'm pregnant.

BD: Let's get married, because I'm not down with paying child support.

BM: Is that supposed to be some sort of proposal?

New Year's Plans or Nah?

BM: Hey. Multiple activities are coming up for New Year's, which falls on your weekend. I *can* count on you to take her on your scheduled weekend, right?

BD: Sure, it just depends on my location, what I got going on that weekend, and what side of town I'm on.

BM: What? ... NEVERMIND.

No Dairy

A child gets dropped off after spending time with the father's family. The mother looks in the bag and notices the to-go snack box is half-filled with mac and cheese. The mother's face drops towards the floor because she had already discussed with the father the importance of not giving their daughter dairy products; she is only 8 months old and the mother's family is lactose intolerant. Everyone in the father's family knows how the mother feels about dairy products.

BM: Hey, remember what we discussed about her not having dairy products?

BD: I don't give her dairy products.

BM: I know you don't, but when your family member dropped her off, I looked in the bag and noticed a container of mac n cheese, which was half-eaten. I asked your family member if they fed her that, and the response was yes. I remember telling them not to give her anything containing milk or cheese; I don't support dairy product intake because of her age. I have told you about my family having a history of lactose intolerance. This is the reason why she was drinking soy formula when she was on the bottle.

BD: This is my family, and my family can do what they want to. Besides, they will take the best care of her. When she is with me, she flows with how we roll. You can't dictate everything!!

A few days later, the child is in the hospital for blood in her stool because of constipation and a change in her normal eating habits.

Unscented

Soaps, Lotions, Deodorants,
Every lady is different.
Every woman is different.
Every mother is different.
We all have our favorite soaps, lotions and
deodorants.

(Baby mama calls baby daddy's cell phone. He hears it ringing, but his girlfriend is within arm's reach of the phone, so he asks her to answer it.)

BM: Hello. I was calling to speak with Vic to ask him why is her skin so red and full of rashes? Did you all use something different on her over the weekend? Did you use a different kind of soap?

Girlfriend: No. But I did put some of my lotion on her after she had her bath yesterday evening.

BM: What kind of lotion did you use?

Girlfriend: My favorite product is Oil of Olay.

BM: Ok that is fine, but is it unscented?

Girlfriend: No, you don't want her to smell good?

BM: It's not about the fragrance at all. She has sensitive skin and she is allergic to fragrant products. I explained this to you the first weekend I let her come over there.

Girlfriend: When I put the lotion on her, she didn't seem to be itching, and her skin didn't look

72

irritated to me. I think you are just trying to start an argument and want everything your way.

BM: Ok, let me send you her doctor records to show you she receives a prescription each year for hydrocortisone cream due to eczema since you think this is a joke or game.

Some may ask why the girlfriend would choose to conflict with the biological mother for a child she only sees a few days out of the month. However, the real question here is, why hasn't the father stepped in to tell the girlfriend not to use those items on their daughter when he knows she has an allergic reaction to fragrant products.

*
* * *

It's none of her business where our child is during my weekend visitation.

* * *
*

Girlfriend saga II

*S*ome weekends will lead into certain Monday holidays like Memorial Day. When problems arise with baby mamas and baby daddies, some baby daddies will use the attorney general's paperwork as a guide, and as a power trip. Since the baby daddy loves to use this to his advantage, it is then a baby mama's duty to remind him of some of the rules that should be followed within the document.

(Doorbell rings the Sunday before Memorial Day-BM opens the door.)

Girlfriend: How are you? *(Attempts to return child to mother)*

BM: I'm great, but tomorrow is a holiday, and Eric is supposed to keep Erica until tomorrow evening.

Girlfriend: I didn't know that.

BM: You're the one that sat down with him to help him understand his rights according to the paperwork, but I guess you just happened to miss that part of the document.

Girlfriend: Well, you are her mother, and I have to work tomorrow.

BM: Well, that is not my problem. What you should do is call Eric and drop her off over there because I am busy as well.

(BM closes the door, and a few hours later, the phone rings.)

BD: What is your problem? Why are you always making things difficult and causing problems?

BM: You told me that you want to have Erica on all days and times presented in the documents. So you are not going to pick and choose.

(BD hangs phone up in BM's face.)

Is baby mama wrong?

*

***

Why should I have to pay child support for 30 days during the summer while the child is with me?

***

*

Tricky Conversations

When I married my husband, I never thought we would ever get a divorce, or he would leave me and the children. That was not in anyone's plan. My husband and I were married for 10 years. During those 10 years, I gave birth to four children. When we started having problems within our marriage, my husband felt the need to step outside the marriage for comfort and love. The sad part is that his family, who claim to be Christians, knew that he was cheating on me and assisted him with his behavior.

He didn't have a problem throwing this woman in my face. Despite this, I felt it was ok to let him go since he wanted this woman. I never worked during the marriage because I was a stay-at-home mom and took care of the children who were all under the age of 6. He and I discussed the financial basis for child support. He agreed to pay me one thousand dollars per month for the children, and of course, I felt that was not enough. But in the end, I was tired of fighting and arguing with him, so I agreed to the payment discussed.

When we arrived at court, he and I talked for a bit in a peaceful manner. When we walked into the court room, I felt it was going to be a smooth moment, quick and easy. The judge asked my ex-husband about paying child support. He expressed to the judge that he wanted full custody of the children because I was not financially able to take care of them. I felt like I was having a nightmare and was about to wake up from this bad dream.

The judge asked me if I was financially able to take care of the children, and of course, I told the judge I was not working. My ex and I had agreed, off the record, that he'd give me one thousand dollars per month in child support, and I would look for a job.

My ex-husband said he never had this conversation with me, and the judge granted him custody of our children. I couldn't believe he would do this to me. When he did that, I wanted to kill him. It was bad enough he cheated on me, and to make matters worse, he did it in front of our children and his family. It seems no one felt the need to correct his actions.

I was granted visitation every other weekend with our children, and it broke my heart to let them go home with their dad and his wife. I knew God was going to guide me and help me through this. After my children were with their dad for six months, the children came to visit me. When they came to visit, two of our boys had bruises all over their legs as if someone had spanked them. So I asked them what happened and they said that daddy's wife beat them because they ate dessert before eating dinner.

I wanted to kill that woman, but I had to play smart and handle things from the legal perspective. I took pictures of my kids, sent them home to their dad, and called CPS. When I sent them home, I received a mysterious call from my ex-husband saying he felt the children needed to be back with me. He didn't go into detail, but I just listened to him and decided not to respond because I really didn't know where he was coming from. I let him know we needed to go through the court system to do it right and that he should be ashamed of himself.

The court date was set, and a mysterious thing happened that was out of anyone's control. My ex-husband worked for the light company and had to climb electric poles during the day. When he climbed one of the poles all the way to the top, he felt some type of electrical shock, which caused him to fall. He hit his head on a rock and was in a coma for weeks. Even though the two of us were going through a battle over the children, I would never want them to see their father hurt, let alone in a coma. When he was hooked up to the machine at the hospital, I decided to bring the children to the hospital to see him. His wife was still on some craziness, and we were not allowed to see him.

If it was up to her, the plug would have been pulled immediately because she was eager to not have to worry about him. Finally, the plug was pulled, my children were returned to me, and we have been happy ever since. My children love and miss their father, and I have forgiven him, trying my best to be a good mother. I wonder what life would have been like if he was still alive. This seems to always enter my thoughts as the children grow into adulthood.

Girlfriend Saga III

Who is the better mother?????

Girlfriend: I hope you like the name-brand clothes and shoes I purchased for your son.

BM: Thanks. I don't shop for things like that, however, it's cool and I appreciate it.

Girlfriend: Is it not your style, or is it because you can't afford the items?

BM: Why would you think that is a question deserving of an answer for a child that I gave birth to?

Girlfriend: It's obvious you can't afford these items because he is always wearing basic t-shirts and jeans. So, if you want him to dress better, I can help you with this.

(BM really marinates on the disrespect given to her by the girlfriend and can't figure out how someone like her, a single mother of two children, would talk down on her as a BM.)

(When she returns to pick up the child, she drops a bag of name-brand clothes off to add insult to injury.)

Girlfriend: Here are some more clothes I picked up this past week for him.

BM: No thank you.

Girlfriend: Why is everything a battle? You should appreciate someone who is willing to give you clothes to help you since you can't do it. My boyfriend gives you enough child support money for you to purchase these items, but you of course, have to use it on things that have nothing to do with the child.

BM: You know what? You're right. Thank you so much for the clothes.

(She takes clothes to orphanage and passes them out to the children in need.)

(The phone rings two months later.)

BD: Why are you not sending him in the items my girlfriend purchased for him?

BM: Because I gave them away.

Ohhhhh well!!!!!

*

**

I don't have full custody, but why can't I have the same amount of control and decision making as the mother?

**

*

Summertime Savings

My baby daddy doesn't have custody, but he follows the paperwork perfectly when it comes to visitation. I commend all fathers who pick up their children for a complete summer, but the question is; are you picking up the child for love or for show?

My baby daddy is a trip in my opinion. My daughter started working for the first time at the children's museum, and as her mother, I was truly excited. She stayed with her father off and on during the summer because he was working two jobs, and still needed my help in regards to transportation including help with her sister.

Her father helped her get an account set up so she can have her check directly deposited into it. When school started, our child wanted me to purchase something for her. I didn't mind doing it, of course, but I asked her to use some of the money from her summer job. She told me she couldn't use it because her father said 'No'.

I didn't mind nor care that her father told her this. But what I didn't understand, was why she didn't have direct access to the account, being that he is the non-custodial parent and doesn't have full custody? When I called him about it, he said this was his decision, he was in control, and there was nothing I could do about it. I guess he was happy that he found something he thought he could control.

I didn't make a big deal about it. However, he doesn't see her crying and wanting to have access to at least some of her money since she worked hard for it. Our daughter is upset, but afraid to confront him about it because she feels she is unable to communicate with him on subjects like this.

Whenever I try to communicate with him to gain clarity and understanding in regards to his decision, he gets on a defensive power trip. She is a great kid and has shown that she can be trusted with money. Shouldn't she be able to at least reward herself with something? I just don't get it.

Deadly Consequences

As an adult I looked back and realized the mistakes that I made, and I feel these mistakes were due to the lack of love shown to me by my father. When I was a little girl, I remember my parents getting a divorce. I was so hurt because I didn't understand the full definition of "divorce". How I came to understand it was based on the fact that my father was no longer in the house, and he would come pick me up every few months. I hated my mother so much because I remember my parents arguing and my father telling my mother he was not in love with her anymore, and there was nothing she could do about it. As a young child, I took that to mean it was my mother's fault.

Middle school years came upon me fast, and I recall seeing my father during my elementary days a few times each year. In middle school, I wanted to be just like my father. He played the trumpet. When I was able to get my hands on a trumpet in middle school, I practiced day and night. I called my father to tell him that I was going to follow in his footsteps. But when I called, a woman answered the phone, and I could hear children in the background. I asked her if I could speak to my father.

She replied, "Hello, so good to hear your voice. I have heard so much about you these last few months." I felt so hurt because I hadn't seen my father within the last three months and I'd never heard anything about her.

The way I saw it, my father was entertaining another woman, and on top of that, she had kids. I, of course, didn't respond to this. I again asked if I could speak to my father. She then let me know that he was out of town on business. My heart just dropped because I didn't know my father worked out of the state, and let alone that he had someone move in, allowing her to answer his phone.

My father returned my phone call when he arrived back in the city.

When he called, he said, "Hey baby girl. How are you? Tiffany let me know you called. Is everything okay with you?"

Instead of me telling him how I really felt, I immediately responded, "I'm good...Hey daddy! I am now learning how to play the trumpet. Can you come and get me so I can show you how well I am doing?"

He responded, "Sure I can do that, I will come and pick you up this weekend. As a matter of fact, I will come Saturday morning at 9:00a.m."

Oh my goodness! I felt so good because my father was coming to pick me up! We would spend the day together, and he could hear me play the tunes I learned on my trumpet. My mother woke up that morning to prepare breakfast. I was so excited that I couldn't eat anything. I looked at the clock in the kitchen and saw it was 8:45 a.m., so I went to the door and waited; I wanted to be ready to run out of the house when he arrived. As I was sitting there for an hour, I figured he was just running late or got stuck in traffic (even though he lived 30 minutes away). Maybe he is picking up a gift to surprise me, I thought to myself. Anything to keep from thinking he wasn't coming.

Eventually, it was evening. My mother kept coming out and telling me to call him. But I felt like I didn't need to do this. I went to my room and started crying, so my mother wouldn't see me in pain over someone she has a negative opinion of. I know this because she speaks about him when her friends call to talk about their children's fathers. The following Monday, I went to school and acted like nothing happened.

The following Wednesday, my father called me to say hello, so I asked him what happened last Saturday and why didn't he come to pick me up.

He replied, "Oh baby girl, I was so busy with helping Tiffany that I lost track of time. But, I will make it up to you."

I could only respond with, "Ok and I love you daddy, but I have to go, so I will talk to you later."

Before I knew it, the end of the year had come. I had joined the jazz band at school, which meant I would move into the next year as a performer for upcoming events.

My own father didn't care to call to check on me or anything. So of course, I reached out to him a whole year later, and I said, "Daddy I have a show that I will be doing for the Thanksgiving festival and I want you to come."

Of course, he let me know he would be in attendance. And you know what? He showed up. I was so shocked, but I was also happy. As he sat in the audience, I zoomed in on him. Even though the lights were out, I was able to focus on him, and I played my heart out.

After the show was over, my father came up to me and I gave him a big hug.

He said, "Man, you have grown!"

I didn't know how to take that. As we were talking, a woman walks up with her two daughters, and he introduced Tiffany as his wife and the two as his step daughters. In my mind, I wanted to kill them because my heart was broken. Tiffany looked like a million dollars, and her children looked like celebrity kids. I have never seen so many diamonds on one lady in my life. She grabbed me as if she had known me forever. As she was hugging me, I felt like this woman and her children didn't feel like I should have been part of the ceremony, let alone find out about his marriage after my concert?

Of course, my mother was in the background, looking at me with a facial expression that said it was going to be okay.

She said to me, "This is just a moment. You are strong and you will get over it."

From that moment on, I knew I had to become tough. But deep down, I didn't feel I was able to do this. I could in front of my mother, but she was the only person I could do this in front of.

A few months passed and my father finally showed up at my doorstep to pick me up. This time, I wasn't ready, and I was shocked he waited on the couch for me. I didn't even ask where we were going. I was just so happy that he came on his own to make time for me. As we were riding, he tells me that he and Tiffany had divorced, and he needed to be alone for a while. I didn't say anything right away, but in the back of my mind I was thinking, wow, he divorced her? My father divorced Tiffany a few days after my concert. As I was listening to him, I became very excited because I was sure my father must have realized he needed to give me more time and that is why he came. Keep in mind, Tiffany was only half his age, so I figured it didn't work because she could pass for my big sister.

My father took me to dinner, and we sat and talked for about thirty minutes. In walked Sheila. My father stood up, then gave her a kiss and a big hug. Earlier, when my father came to pick me up, he just smiled, kissed me on the cheek, and said, "Come on."

As I was sitting there, I realized that my father didn't come pick me up to spend time with me. In fact, he picked me up for another reason. Why was it that I could not have my father to myself? Why couldn't my father put me first? And the woman looked like she could have been Tiffany's sister. What was it with my father and these young-looking women? Then, Sheila sat down and started talking. Before I knew it, the conversation was between the two of them, and I was just sitting there.

I tried tuning them out by listening to what my dad had on the radio, but then I heard the wrong thing, I mean, the most disrespectful thing in the world to me at that time. My father asked this woman to marry him. My eyes got big and watery. Of course, the two of them thought I was excited about their engagement, and that was definitely not it. My heart was so broken. Did my father feel that this time he wanted me to be part of the process since he didn't include me in the last time he asked someone to marry him?

On the ride home, I sat in the backseat of the car since Sheila was in the front. This was a horrible moment and a heart-destructive feeling. When I was attempting to get out the car, I figured my father would have walked me to the door to tell me he loved me and to thank me for coming.

Instead, he reached back with his hand as I was opening the car door to say, "I love you baby girl and I will see you soon." As he was gesturing his goodbyes with his hand, Sheila said, "It was great meeting you." When I got out the car, I had to really get it together quickly before my mother could see my face.

Like the old saying expresses, 'you can fool some people some of the time, but you can never fool your mama'. I ran upstairs to my room and just cried. My mother came in the room and asked me what was wrong.

I replied, "You know daddy has the same story all over again." She just grabbed me and hugged me, but her hugs and love couldn't end the pain that was piercing in my heart. I just couldn't understand why my father would do me like that. What kind of a father treats his child that way? Of course I got over it and moved on.

In high school, I joined the marching band. I was so excited because my father was in the marching band when he was in high school and college. I knew my father would attend all football games because it was the high school he attended, at least that is what I thought. The first game of the season came, and I texted my father to give him the full season's schedule. He replied that he would make all the games, and he was so proud of me.

When halftime was over, I sat back in the stands and turned around to see if my father was at the game. I saw my mother, but I didn't see my father. I didn't think anything of it because when I was a little girl, my father brought me to the games with him, and he never walked around.

When we were finally able to take a ten-minute restroom break, I used that time to look around for my father, and I didn't see him. As I was riding the bus back to the school, I wanted to cry, but of course I couldn't do that in front of my classmates or my band director. My mother was there to pick me up, and I asked her if she saw daddy. She quickly let me know with the sarcastic question, "What you think?!"

I was upset. I texted him and asked him, where was he? He replied an hour later and told me he was running late from work, so he decided to go for drinks with his wife instead. In the back of my mind, I couldn't help but wonder; why he couldn't at least come to see me perform for halftime before going to get drinks? He texted me to let me know he would come and get me that Saturday morning which was the next day. I just replied, ok. I didn't expect for him to come, but he did. He showed up with his wife, but it was not Sheila; it was a lady named Meagan.

When my dad arrived, he was driving a minivan because Meagan had three kids, one who happened to be in high school. I couldn't help but notice her daughter in the backseat, and I climbed in to sit next to her. As Meagan started saying her hellos, she introduced me to her daughter Patrice. Patrice and I looked at one another as if we were inspecting each other from head to toe.

Patrice informed me that her school won their football game last night and then the family went out to eat together. Since we were in the far back of the van, where my father and her mother were not able to hear our conversation, she told me that my father went to her game and supported her marching during half time. I smiled, but I wanted to jump across the seat and fight my father. My father lied to me and didn't feel bad about doing it.

That entire day, we hung out with his wife and her children at the mall. My father didn't talk with me, hug me, or express any interest. I wondered why my father would even come and pick me up. He never called me and if he did, it was just to involve me with some other woman or just to say he was in my life when he really wasn't. He didn't care anything about me, and the sad part is, I don't know what I did to him for him to treat me like that.

He dated younger women and put their children first as if I didn't exist. My feelings were hurt, and I kept allowing him to hurt me. I asked my mother to come pick me up while we were at the mall. When she arrived, he said to my mother, "Hey is this is a coincidence, you being at the mall the same time we are?"

My mother replied, "No, our daughter called to be picked up, so I am here." My father looked at me and asked me why I did that. I let him know that

93

I had forgotten that I had rehearsal for the Christmas show, which, of course, was a lie.

He said, "Oh, ok you could have told me that and we could have dropped you off."

I whispered under my breath, "That's a bunch of bull but whatever."

Patrice heard and gave me a blank stare. The ride home with my mother was in pure silence. My mother finally said with a strong voice, "You need to figure out how to tell your father how you truly feel." We pulled up in the driveway, and I just ran into the house and went to sleep.

I had gotten used to my father not being around, but I started having bad thoughts of him, like I couldn't care less if he died. Even though I loved him, I was starting to hate him at the same time. During the Christmas holidays, I decided to go to my father's to be the bigger person and tell him how I truly felt. When I knocked on the door, a young lady answered the door and asked me who I was.

I started seeing red and lots of it. I screamed, "His daughter!"

Before I knew it, I had placed my hands around her neck and just choked her until she was unable to breathe. While I was doing it, I could only see my father's face and before I knew it, I killed her. All I could do is run out of the apartment complex, jump in my mother's car, and go straight home as if nothing had happened. I went straight to bed, and eventually the police knocked on the front door asking my mother where I was.

When the police came to my room, they placed me under arrest for murder. During questioning, the police asked me questions in front of some lawyer, and I didn't answer anything because I was zoned out. Since I didn't answer any questions and I was still considered a juvenile, I was placed in a cell by myself. After a few days of sitting in my cell, my father showed up. He walked in, and I turned my back to him.

The first thing he uttered was, "Why did you kill her?" I still refused to answer him because at that point I hated him with all my being. He came to me, grabbed me, and turned me around. He began to shake me and asked question after question, "Why would you do something like that? What is wrong with you? Why are you looking like that around the eyes and what is going on with you?"

A few days went by, and a therapist came into the cell along with a psychologist. I would not talk to them or speak with them about why I did it. Finally, my mother was asked to come in with the psychologist and said, "You will feel better if you just tell the truth."

I allowed one teardrop to fall and said, *"She didn't know who I was and she should have known."*

Did you forget about

ME

for Father's Day since

YOU

are playing Daddy to someone else's

KIDS?

Dance with My Father

*W*hen I entered high school, my relationship with my father was pretty much nonexistent. By this time, I had already gotten used to the fact that he was married to someone that wasn't my mother. When I was a little girl, the only times I would hear from my father was every other weekend.

My father was the type that only came around to impress everyone, making it look like he was "involved daily". As a little girl, he only came to pick me up to show his family he was a great "every other weekend" father. Once I entered junior high, those visits became less and less. In high school, I found other things to keep me occupied, and one of those things happened to be dancing on the Mighty Eagle Dance Team. Every year, our school had a Daddy Daughter Dance during the halftime show of the Homecoming football game. Since I hadn't spent time with my father in a few months, the dance was a perfect opportunity for him and me to rebuild and catch up.

I was really shocked when my father agreed to be my dance partner. During rehearsals, I felt my father and I become closer to one another. We had to rehearse every day to make sure he memorized all the steps. I almost didn't want the rehearsals to end because this was the most time that I had spent with my dad in such a long time. While learning this new dance routine, I felt like we were also learning a new way to communicate, and this brought us even closer.

The day before the show, my father came to pick me up from my mother's home to take me to dinner. While we were there, he told me he was so proud of me, and that was the first time I felt like my father was real and honest with me and not doing things to impress others. Hearing my dad say those words, reassured me how much he loved me and wouldn't let me down.

The day of the event, I could hardly contain my excitement. I waited down by the gate for him to arrive in anticipation. It was ten minutes before the half time show, and still my father was nowhere to be found.

This was not like him at all. Usually he would call and speak on why he was absent. Since my father did not show, I was unable to dance in the halftime performance. I didn't cry right then. I had to hold in my emotions because I didn't want to bring any extra attention on myself. Strangely, I didn't receive a call from my father until the next day.

He told me that his step daughter had a car accident, and he wasn't able to make the show. I held the phone, and before I started to get upset, I asked my father in a calm tone, "Was her father and your wife there?"

He replied, "Yes."

Knowing that his stepdaughter had both of her parents by her side, I didn't understand why my father couldn't come and do the father-daughter halftime show with me, and then go to the hospital. I really felt my father was being selfish. This was a dance that I had been looking forward to since the day he accepted the invite. I had told all my friends and family about it, and they were all there to see us dance. All my friends at school knew how much this dance meant to me because it was all that I seemed to talk about.

Instead, I was left at the gate, alone, without a father to dance with. I had to face the embarrassment of my classmates asking me what happened and why wasn't my father present.

It's moments like those that caused me to push away from my dad. It seemed that every time I got close to him and started to believe in him, he would put someone else before me.

*
***

Should the child have the father's last name if the mother and father were never together as a union, but made a beautiful child together?

***
*

All in Your Approach: Confession II

Therapist: What is going on with your daughter?

BM: She is acting out in school, and I am so tired and stressed because of it.

Therapist: Did you find out why?

BM: When I talked to her, she said she is tired of going to visit her father, because she can never have one-on-one time with him. She feels her time with her father always consists of his family and whichever woman is his girlfriend at the time.

Therapist: What advice did you give her?

BM: I told her she didn't have to go over there anymore, and she is of age to make certain decisions for herself.

Therapist: Have you ever thought about how this would make her father feel?

BM: Why should I care? He doesn't care about spending quality time with her.

Therapist: To you this may be true, but he probably doesn't feel he is wrong. Maybe you should approach him and see where he is coming from, and find a way for his daughter to be able to tell him her feelings. Sometimes offering the moment of one-on-one can be done easily by saying, "Hey Daddy, can just the two of us go skating this weekend?"

BM: I never thought about it that way. I will speak with my daughter and tell her to confront her father in this manner.

If the child lives with the mother 90% of the time and visits the father 10% of the time, should decisions for the child be equally divided?

6 Kids Later

$\mathscr{I}$ have witnessed a baby daddy who walked off on six jobs simply because he didn't like it. Keep in mind, he has kids to pay child support for, and my son is baby number six. When it comes to health insurance for all his kids, he feels that he should pay one standard price. For example: if health insurance is three hundred and fifty dollars each month, he feels he should be able to divide that amount by six kids, and that should cover health insurance for all.

I work over forty hours a week. I have to take our son to school every morning. Later in the day, I leave my job to pick him up from school, just to take him to after school care so that I can wrap up my day at work.

My baby daddy doesn't have a car so I have to drop our child off to him for visitation. To make matters worse, he doesn't believe in having only one or two of his kids. Instead, he wants all of them at the same time; if one cancels, then he will cancel with all of the children after he had already told them that they could come.

My baby daddy and I decided on the amount I should get per month when he keeps a job, which was four hundred dollars when our son was two years old. I hadn't received any child support in two years, and finally he decided to get a job, which is always a good thing. When he went down to the child support office to set everything up, the child support office had a set amount to deduct for each child. Mine came out to be four hundred and forty dollars per month. He had the nerve to call and ask me if I could give him forty dollars a month back because we agreed upon four hundred dollars. Keep in mind, this was an agreement made when our child was two years old. This is what I go through with my baby daddy.

*You're upset with me
as your son, for praising
my mother's husband
on Father's Day,
but I only hear from
you on Father's Day?*

Happy Father's Day

"Happy Father's Day to all the Mothers doing it themselves..."

There are many single mothers out here who know the whereabouts of their child's or children's fathers. Many people say, I would find him and make him be a father; I would not allow him to not be in the child's life. Some will even go to say that you are a fool for letting him get away with not taking care of his children. The above expression should really be thought of and spoken with care. Not only does the mother have to deal with being the only parent, she also has to deal with her friends and family speaking about a subject that they don't have to go through.

As a single mother, it is your responsibility to provide food, clothing, and shelter for your child or children, regardless if you receive support from the father or not. So the above statements and opinions from others state that you are also responsible for teaching a man who engaged in consensual intercourse, how to be a father, by doing whatever you can to make him be part of the child's life. If you don't, then you are looked at by other women, friends, family, or other people as a horrible mother because you didn't make *HIM* be part of a life he created.

So the questions posed to many single mothers are: Why should we glorify these type of men on Father's Day? Why should we give recognition or teach our children to bring praise and respect to fathers who they barely know? Why should we, as the full time mothers, who do all the work, not accept "Father's" Day cards from our children, who seem to recognize that we are doing the job that is meant for two people?

Some women say there are men out here making children with multiple women, and they are doing nothing to provide support within the homes that these children live. Instead of asking why men keep making babies with different women, you hear many people ask why a woman would get pregnant from a man that has multiple kids from different women.

But since the baby is here, one would expect that a man would want to provide. When he doesn't, the ball is completely in your court, every day, which includes Father's Day. I see many men on the internet who post pictures of their children on Father's Day. But if you speak with the mothers, they will tell you that the children barely see their fathers. These fathers don't pay child support, but they want the public to believe they are actually involved on a full-time basis. They comment negatively on the mother, saying she is this and she is that. Soon after, comes all the disrespectful comments from strangers who really don't know you and what you do; they only know what is posted for the public.

Many great fathers who are doing their job don't understand why a single mother should get love and respect on the day that is set aside for fathers.

108

The term is 'great father'. What is the definition of a great father? Some men feel they are great fathers since they make a point to show up every other weekend because the Attorney General tells them that every other weekend is father time. Some great fathers feel that because they pay child support every month, it qualifies them to be labeled a great father. However, the question is, would you give the child support monthly if you were not FORCED to do so?

Some men feel they are great fathers because they pay health insurance every month. The question is, if you were not FORCED to pay the health insurance, would you pay it? They spend money on the kids, but the clothes, accessories and items are not allowed to be sent back home since child support is being provided, and this means they are 'great fathers'.

As a single mother, I hear and see fathers talk about and post pictures of their children and their successes all over the internet. But is this a true image of what is displayed? Or is this what the father wants everyone to see? Some fathers work six days each week, but many single mothers work six days each week as well. Many fathers say they have to work and do what they have to do, and the child has to understand that. What if single mothers said the same thing in the same way and acted in the same manner as the non-custodial parent? How would that make the child feel? Both can't be absent. Both want equal rights. But are both doing equal work?

The question goes back to: why should some mothers be acknowledged on Father's Day?

She's My Dad Too

$\mathcal{I}$am 20 years old and married with a set of twins. Having these twins really helped me to realize how much my father wasn't there for me. In no way am I saying my father didn't love me or that he wasn't in my life, but I see the difference between me and my other siblings.

My father and my mother separated when I was very young. He would come and pick me up every other weekend. I didn't know what that was about because having a child's mind, I thought my father would come and see me every day since he lived with us every day.

Since this wasn't the case, I didn't make a big deal about it because he made the effort to come and pick me up. My father left when I was 3 years old and he came every other weekend for two years. When Father's Day would come around, he would pick me up on the Thursday before Father's Day Sunday. We would always head to Galveston Beach and stay the entire day. We would walk the beach, play in the dirty water, play baseball on the sand, and eat at various restaurants because he knew I loved fish. I looked forward to every Father's Day.

Then, when I turned 5, my father remarried. Not only did he remarry, he married a woman with six kids. I was really excited because I would have other kids to play with when I went over to his house. I was so wrong. My father continued to pick me up every other weekend, but things were really different. I guess that is to be expected, but I was sure the Father's Day weekend wouldn't change at all.

I called my father when I was 6 years old to ask him what time was he coming to pick me up that Thursday before Father's Day weekend. My father told me that he was going out of town with his wife and her children to visit her family in another state because they were doing a big family Father's Day event.

I started crying so hard when I hung up the phone because I felt like my father didn't have to go, or he could have at least taken me with them. For the next three years, my father never made it a priority to come and pick me up for Father's Day weekend, and the every-other-weekend pickups started to decrease. By the time I made it to middle school, he and I talked more on the phone than we saw each other, and even that wasn't a daily occurrence. After a while, I realized the only person spending quality time with me was my mother. So after that, I stopped giving my father recognition for Father's Day and made sure to glorify my mother every day, including Father's Day.

*
***

So what if I am not married to her, the child should have my last name.

***
*

Daddy-Daughter Luncheon

At the age of 30, I can finally speak on this subject; I stayed very reclusive for years and felt it was my fault for not having a close relationship with my father. When I was born, my father was (and still is) married to the woman with whom he cheated on with my mother. My mother never mentioned my father at all to me. The subject never came up because growing up in a small town, nothing was a secret, except to children.

When my mother enrolled me in school for kindergarten, I was approached by a teacher who always spoke to me and called me Cherry. I always corrected her and told her my name was Melissa. She finally introduced me to the little girl that I resembled, who was a year older than me. I had to admit the two of us looked alike. So when my mother came to pick me up from school, I wanted my mother to see this little girl and see how much she and I resembled. When my mother saw her, I introduced them and the little girl said, "My name is Cherry Woods."

My mother grabbed my hand and rushed out of the school. When we got in the car, I told my mother that she wasn't being very nice. My mother took me to McDonald's to sit me down in the play area to speak with me. My mom knew how much I loved McDonald's. My mother told me that Cherry was my sister. She tried to explain to me in the best way she could, that she had slept with a married man. She explained that because of this, my father didn't want to have anything to do with me. He needed me to remain a secret so that his marriage wouldn't be messed up.

I started to cry because I knew nothing of my father. I had never understood why all the other kids had dads, and I didn't. But to know I actually had a sibling really made me smile. However, that smile quickly turned into a saddened heart because I realized I couldn't tell her she was my sister. As much as I wanted to, I remembered my mother had already told me not to because she didn't want people to treat me differently because of it.

That same year, the school had a father and daughter's day luncheon for all grade levels. Although Cherry and I attended the same school, Cherry was a year older than me. Because we were in different grade levels, we didn't have the same lunch hour. As I heard the lunch bell ring, I immediately asked my teacher if I could go to the restroom, because it was an emergency. Without hesitation, she let me go and I was ecstatic, because I really wanted to see who my father was and what he looked like. When I saw him, I envisioned myself in Cherry's place like a fantasy that would never come true; deep in my heart, though, I wished it would.

I was standing at the end of the table looking at them as they smiled and gazed at one another with love in their eyes. It was at that moment that I really wished I could trade places with Cherry, or at least, share that moment with my dad. I was so lost in the moment that I didn't even hear the principal calling my name. The principal tapped me on my shoulder and asked me why I wasn't in class. I told her I wanted to see Cherry and tell her how pretty she looked today. This wasn't my real reason, but at the moment it was all I could come up with. The principal walked me back to class.

Cherry and I stayed friends throughout the years. One day, while we were in middle school, she invited me to her house after school. This was my golden opportunity to meet my dad again and get an even closer look at him.

My mother didn't know of my plans to go over Cherry's house because she worked late. I remember feeling excited and nervous at the same time. I approached the door and stood there for a few seconds, which felt like an eternity. As I was about to ring the doorbell, the door swung open, and Cherry greeted me with a huge smile. Before rushing back up the stairs, she told me to go towards the living room. When I sat down on the couch, I met her older brothers who were in high school, meaning they were my brothers as well. I couldn't help but notice the resemblance between us all. I thought to myself, "Wow, I have brothers too."

I immediately felt faint, as my father walked in, grinning from ear to ear as he greeted Cherry and her brothers. I stood there hoping that he'd notice a resemblance. I was scared, excited and sad at the same time. Before he made his way up the stairs and out of sight, Cherry asked her dad to be sure to be home on Sunday at 1:00p.m. because she and her brothers had a surprise for him on Father's Day. He agreed to be home, and all I could seem to think about was how was I going to be able to be here on Sunday too.

I begged Cherry to let me come over for Father's Day, so she did. I was so excited to see my dad again that I could hardly compose myself. I

115

picked out my best outfit and made sure that I looked my best. If I received a chance to get his attention, I wanted to look my best. I told my mother I wanted to ride my bike around the neighborhood that day and she allowed me to go without any questions since that was something I did almost every day. I rode my bike to their home for Father's Day and sat at the dinner table; again, I started fantasizing.

I was sitting at the table with Cherry, her three brothers, and her parents. Her father, my father, started speaking on how much of a blessing all of his kids were, how he would not be where he was if he didn't have them, and how he would make sure they were all successful and financially secure.

Briefly, I felt like I was a part of the moment, but within a blink of an eye, I was snapped out of that fantasy. My daydreaming was quickly broken when my father asked me why I wasn't spending Father's Day with my own father. At that moment, I almost choked on the lump in my throat.

I took a deep breath, swallowed my emotions, and responded, "Because he cheated on my mother and didn't want to include me in family functions." I walked away from the table and left.

As I was riding my bike home that Sunday afternoon, I realized I would never honor that man on Father's Day or any other day.

Showtime

My parents are not together, and like other children, I dreamed of a family with just the four of us together. My brother was a year younger than I, and we have the same mother and father. Since I was a little girl, I have always wanted to be on stage acting. Both parents always encouraged me to be the best and never give up on my dreams. I have been in over one hundred plays, cast as the main character or sometimes just an extra. The funny thing is, I never saw my father at any of my productions, and I finally decided to tell him how I felt. I expressed to him how I did not like the fact that he never would come to any of my shows. My father apologized for not being there and reassured me on how much he loved me.

After that conversation, he made me a promise and told me he would not miss any more of my shows. Not long thereafter, I was offered a part in a production. This production would be my biggest yet. This production would be in front of an audience of eight thousand people. I told my mother and my father, and they both said they would be there. I spoke with the director, and he gave me three free tickets for my family.

I was so excited. Every week, I made sure to speak with my father before rehearsals. He spoke to me with the best encouraging words. His words were filled with so much love and admiration that at times, I almost came to tears.

The week before the production, my father introduced my brother and me to his new girlfriend. She seemed really sweet, and I was happy to see my father found someone as nice as she was. We all hung out on that Sunday, nearly a week before my show that upcoming Saturday night. When the night of production came, it was hard to see in the audience because it was so dark. When I did my final bow and went to the dressing room, I had to immediately go out to the lounge to greet my fans as well as my family. When I walked out to the lounge, my father wasn't anywhere to be found. I quickly scanned the lobby in search for him, but I still could not find him. As I was walking away from the group of actors that shared in the production with me, I saw my mother, my brother, and my father's girlfriend.

This was a bit confusing to me. I didn't quite understand why my dad was not in attendance when he promised me that he would not miss another one of my performances. When I called him to ask him why he didn't make it, he told me his girlfriend wanted to go, and he didn't want to disappoint her, so he gave her the ticket. Seemingly so, he was more concerned with disappointing his new girlfriend than he was in disappointing me. After that, I was totally done with my father.

My mother is there for me
everyday.
She takes off work,
helps me with my homework,
And is always available
When I need her.
So when Father's Day comes
Around, I add this day to
My other days of praising my
mother!

No Hard Feelings

I am 16 years old and I grew up without a father. My mother worked five days each week, and on the weekends, she devoted time to me by placing me in baseball, basketball, and football. As a young boy, I didn't understand it. Now that I am older, I really understand and appreciate her for this. She wasn't able to teach me to be a man, but she tried her hardest to keep me out of trouble and wanted me to complete school, as well as make a future for myself.

When I attended the football, baseball, and basketball camps, I met so many other boys whose fathers were active and always there to support. Instead of falling into a trap of depression, I decided to get to know these boys and get to know their fathers as well. From this, I grew up with many fathers, but not the father I wanted.

I really wanted to have a relationship with my father. But because he didn't like my mother and she didn't abort me, he chose to distance himself from me to keep from messing up another relationship that he kept from my mother. I am not upset with him, but every year for Mother's Day and Father's Day, I always give my mother a card. I was told to do this by all the fathers that mentored me. I was told that I needed to understand that my mother is doing the job of two, and she should always be recognized for it.

YOU

want me to acknowledge

YOU

for Father's Day but

YOU

only are my Daddy when it is convenient for

YOU?

Second Choice

$\mathcal{N}$ow that I have reached the age of 18, I can speak on this matter with confidence and strength. My parents divorced when I was only 9 years old, and I felt like it was my fault. They argued over things, and some of the arguments were about me. When my father left, he immediately remarried as if he was seeing this woman while he was still with my mother. I don't have proof, and I would not dare ask my mother.

When my father lived with us, he took me to baseball, basketball, football, soccer and hockey games every year. We were not poor, but we were definitely not rich. When my father left, I just knew all the things we did together wouldn't stop. Wow, was I wrong!

My father remarried after divorcing my mom. One day, I called him to ask him about going to a baseball game. He told me he would take me and would let me know when the game was. I didn't understand that visitation was something involved with divorce. Since my father was not there at all after the age of 9, I thought he would come and pick me up regularly. This never happened. I asked my mother when my daddy was coming to spend time with me. My mother told me to go ahead and call him to set up some dates.

When I called my father to ask him when he was picking me up and what baseball game were we going to, he told me that he was not going to be able to take me to any baseball games because he had to work. He also told me that my mother was taking all of his money, so he needed to get a second job to make ends meet. He failed to tell me that he had another already-made family that he had to provide for.

Of course as a young man, I was angrier with my mother than my father. I felt like she was the reason he didn't have any time to spend with me. He finally came to pick me up. He took me over to his house, and that was the first time I ever met his new wife and her two boys.

As I was walking around the house and looking at the pictures, I noticed a picture of my dad at a baseball game with his new wife and her two boys. I asked my dad when did they take those pictures, and he told me the new company he worked for gave him four tickets to the baseball game. He went on to say that the tickets were given to him at the last minute, and he wasn't able to get an extra ticket.

My heart was so hurt and crushed because he basically said that I was second choice to two children that already had a daddy. When he dropped me off at home, I cried so hard and stayed in my room the rest of the night. From that moment on, my father called me just on holidays and a few weekends. The times after the divorce that I spent with him always had to be shared with his wife and her children. Now that I am an adult, I still don't have a great relationship with my father, but I realized that it was not my mother's fault or mine, and I won't continue to blame myself for his lack of being a father to me.

★

★★★

If you are a father every other weekend, does this make you a single father?

★★★

★

Here's Your Card

My father always came around to pick me up when the entire family came to town. My father paid a great amount in child support monthly and made sure I was taken care of in regards to my medical expenses. I rarely saw my father the majority of the year because he remarried when I was about five years old. He and his wife had kids together as well. He would come and pick me up for family reunions, holiday events, and other family birthday parties. When I was young, I didn't understand, but as I got older, I realized what my father was doing. It had nothing to do with me. It was more of a way to "show off" to everyone that he was this "good dad".

When I turned 13 years old, he came to pick me up for Father's Day. I asked him why he always picked me up for Father's Day weekend.

He replied, "It is the weekend set up especially for me to show how great of a father I am."

So my response to him was, "You feel this day makes you a great father because…"

He quickly cut me off by saying, "I provide for you, and I make sure you are taken care of."

I didn't respond to that comment; I just said, "Okay daddy."

I felt like saying, "You never call me during the week to see how I am doing, you never attend any school events, you only come when there's lots of family members in your presence, and you never come alone to pick me up so we can spend one-on-one time together."

I should give my father a best entertainer of the year award instead of a "Happy Father's Day" card.

Poetry for a Selfish Baby Daddy

Selfish Baby Daddy

So you decide to leave us
Express to your family it's like freedom
Go-ahead with your green light
and have sanction on a sufferance flight

Don't have any choice but to tolerate
you want another woman and a new family

okay

So instead of being a father daily in this home
you choose to:

Maintain
Prepare
Arrange
Cater
Contribute
Look after
Feed
Take care of
Grant

With your new woman and her kids since their
daddy refuses to:

Fix up
Replenish
Lend
Administer
Furnish
Proffer
Minister

So now you feel like a man being a daddy on a daily
to other blood lines
128

other blood lines
other blood lines

-Ablyss

Sex Makes You

You know that light bulbs dream
During winter an imaginative spring

Glow, make your body flow
tell me what you know

Beams of realistic lies
Venom teardrops from your eyes

Where did you actually lay your head last night?
Before I reached a *climax shut eye?*
Where did you actually lay your head last night?

The true image of your love I never knew
Becausssseeeeeeeee
Darkness, bloom yellow roses hydrated by fibbing
expressions

No herbs, no weed, no ganja
but you keep blowing smoke off of I won't

Sex makes you say I want you,
Sex makes you say I love you,
Sex makes you say I want you,
Sex makes you say have my baby,
Sex makes you say I will be here forever

You have my word…
Rise of action, Climax
then I awake to find you are Mr. Vanish.

-Ablyss

Legal Eagle

you're mad I called the legal eagle
attorney generals
because I am in need of advocacy
to receive finances in place of the lack of work you
contribute to me
to raise our baby

My mouthpiece drives you insane
because you would prefer for me to shut up
than put these people in
your life to make you pay up

it's just proxy aka barrister

you will still be a man at the end
when the gavel strikes that wood
paying child support is your new friend
your child is now good

and you still mad I called the legal eagle

-Ablyss

Back Child Support

He didn't consider me. He left me to raise these kids.
All three.
I didn't get a chance to enjoy my youth.
I gave him my innocence.
I gave him my truth.

He played with my emotions
and my feelings
simply to leave me here alone

Am I wrong because I refuse to let him leave me to
raise these kids on my own?

It's bad enough he only comes around on holidays
and every time I send the kids with him,
it seems I have to pay...

He's mad at me because his child support is in
arrears
But who does he think has been taking care of his
kids all these years?

I've shed sweat and tears doing it alone,
but what I refuse to do is,
do it on my own.

He asked me to bear his children, and that I did do.
But now that I am a mother, I had to ask, "Where are
you?"
`
So yes, he has to help out, even if it means that he
has to pay me.

So I decided to tell him this...

132

You want me to wave the arrears
Simply to save you,
but when the kids and I struggled,
I needed you to save me too.

-Onney

I Got This

do what you are supposed to do...
and when you don't I will continue to:

boogie
bunny hop
trip the light
cut a rug
tango
waltz

with you
till you handle your business and help me
provide for our baby

-Ablyss

134

Stipendium

You would rather take our child
than pay child support

Is that why our child is now always with your
mama?

Is that why our child is always with your girlfriend?

You stand in front of a judge and dangle your
dollars,
as if you are better,
but in the end our child sees you the same
amount of time when he was living with me.

You are a selfish person and heartless...
Anything to get out of paying child support

-Ablyss

Unscrupulous Rumors

You think I am dirty,
not well put together smutty
Inside your soul you feel I am unkempt
a foul spirit not heaven sent

You express my house is messy
slight disarray, slovenly untidy
You spread rumors to demean
and paint an image of me as unsanitary

You once adored me
now you hate me
and express how you hate
you had a child from me

But I have a question:

If I am so dirty, why would you have sex with
me unprotected?

-Ablyss

Dusty Toys

your weekends mean just that
as you say

purchase gifts
lovely items
baby boy
wants to show his friends

he can't because what is your weekend toys
stays 1st 3rd and 5th weekend toys

you would rather
control and store
his toys and devices
at your place
to make me look bad
since I can't afford
them in my place

you would rather pile
accumulate
let clothes get too small
agitate
hold back technology devices

just to make me look bad
that's pathetic and sad

-Ablyss

Reflection
"The Liberation of a Brown-Skinned Girl"

I'm on the verge of a break up.
a break up to make up all of the inconsistencies that
I have found within me...
So yes, I am breaking up with myself!
It's not about anyone else,
because when it's all said and done and the trouble
hits the fan,
I am the only one left to take the stand,...
and I understand what bad choices can do.
Bad choices can make you look like the fool,
bad choices can make you seem so uncouth–
I tell you the truth that, I HAVE HAD MY SHARE!!

So as I stand in the mirror, I can't stand to see
the reflection staring back at me.
So it's time that I remove all of the trash and debris,
plus the makeup!
And take up some advice from my old friend 7...
like he said, "it's not about Mary Kay, Fashion Fair or
Mac it's the personal baggage that's attached,"
and I refuse to be the bag lady!!!
So today I am breaking up with me!
Because when I look in that mirror I can't stand the
reflection that I see staring back at me.

Now don't get me wrong
everything I see is not bad,
but it's sad because, as I look beyond the surface of
the reflection and look into my own eyes,
the pain I have inflicted on myself

138

makes me want to cry.

How can I make bad decisions in relationships
and then have the audacity,
to turn around and ask God, why Me?
How can I love a man more than I love myself?
How can I put everything else before my well-being
and put my priorities on a shelf?
It's time to wake up, so I am going to shake up
myself with a personal break-up
so I can be a better me
and be satisfied with the reflection I see
in that mirror staring back at me.

Yes, I am a great mother to my sons,
and I love all three, yes indeed.
But where's the man that planted those seeds?
The problem was I put his wants before my needs!
The problem was I never had time to BREATHE,
a mother at the young age of 16!
Yeah, I may have finished school
but I have disillusioned myself with love
by playing the fool...
Not just once, but twice
so I have to tell myself
that something just ain't right.

You can't do the same thing
expecting different results,
that mathematical equation will never add up.
The problem wasn't them, it was me,
because I allowed those men to treat me unfairly

My first husband beated on me
and my second husband cheated on me
and I stuck around way too long
because I didn't think that I was worthy.
That mindset was embedded in my mentality
leaving me to be
a product of my environment on the inside,
so I wore a smile on the outside
trying to hide my dismay, but today I AM FREE!
I am free from your judgment of me,
I am free to be whomever I want to be,
even if you don't find it satisfactory.

I am breaking up with me because I will no longer be
- bound by the molestation that happened to me
from the dead man I had to call step-daddy,
I will no longer be bound
by extension cord beatings
and mother screaming
YOU B****! YOU AINT GONE BE S***!

I owe it to that little black girl
who was lost in this dark world
a new beginning with a Happy Ending.
SHE DESERVES TO BE FINALLY BE HAPPY.
She deserves a life that's tear free
and full of possibilities.

All my life I have lived just to prove them wrong! I've
written books, songs and recited poems,
starred in stage plays
and executive produced my own CD,
even did a few movies.

140

But still I couldn't seem to break away
from the shackles that held me,
because with all that success I still felt empty.
I still thought that it was my image
that would make me!

But I was sadly mistaken,
because they say imitation
is the best form of flattery,
but not when you're imitating being happy!
Not when your closest friends
turn out to be your enemies.

I would walk through the poetry lounge
with this great big smile,
making sure my hair was on point
and my clothes were in style.
But who the hell cared?
I wasn't content
even when I did get compliments.
That was my get-away
from the reality of dealing with ME,
and so...we're breaking up!

All those things I went through
I never let go and forgot...
I am making up my mind to say
that this isn't what LIFE'S about!

I want to be free...
so I am breaking up with me,
because when I look in the mirror
do you know who I need to see?

I need to see?

A God-Fearing,
Faith-having,
Bold,
Beautiful
and Secure Black Woman
staring back at me!

And that is what I call
A REFLECTION of Perfection...

-Onney

What Is Child Support?

In family law and public policy, **child support** (or **child maintenance**) is an ongoing, periodic payment made by a parent for the financial benefit of a child following the end of a marriage or other relationship. Child maintenance is paid directly or indirectly by an *obligor* to an *obligee* for the care and support of children of a relationship that has been terminated, or in some cases never existed. Often the obligor is a non-custodial parent. The obligee is typically a custodial parent, a caregiver, a guardian, or the state.

Depending on the jurisdiction, a custodial parent may pay child support to a non-custodial parent. Typically one has the same duty to pay child support irrespective of sex, so a mother is required to pay support to a father just as a father must pay a mother. In some jurisdictions where there is joint custody, the child is considered to have two custodial parents and no non-custodial parents, and a custodial parent with a higher income (obligor) may be required to pay the other custodial parent (obligee). In other jurisdictions even with legally shared residence, unless they can prove exactly equal contributions, one parent will be deemed the non-resident parent for child support and will have to pay the other parent a proportion of their income, the "resident" parent's income or needs are not assessed.

In family law, child support is often arranged as part of a divorce, martial separation, annulment, determination of parentage or dissolution of a civil union and may supplement alimony (spousal support) arrangements. The right to child support and the responsibilities of parents to provide such support have been internationally recognized. The 1992 United Nations Convention on the Rights of the Child is a binding convention signed by every member nation of the United Nations and formally ratified by all but South Sudan and the United States. It declares that the upbringing and development of children and a standard of living adequate for the children's development is a common responsibility of both parents and a fundamental human right for children, and asserts that the primary responsibility to provide such for the children rests with their parents. Other United Nations documents and decisions related to child support enforcement include the 1956 New York Convention on the Recovery Abroad of Maintenance created under the auspices of the United Nations, which has been ratified by the 64 of the UN member state.

In addition, the right to child support, as well as specific implementation and enforcement measures, has been recognized by various other international entities, including the Council of
144

Europe, the European Union and the Hague Conference.

Within individual countries, examples of legislation pertaining to, and establishing guidelines for, the implementation and collection of child maintenance include the 1975 Family Law Act(Australia), the Child Support Act (United Kingdom) and the Maintenance and Affiliation Act (Fiji) Child support in the United States, 45 C.F.R. 302.56 requires each state to establish and publish a Guideline that is presumptively correct, and Review the Guideline, at a minimum, every four (4) years. Child support laws and obligations are known to be recognized in a vast majority of world nations, including the majority of countries in Europe, North America and Australasia, as well as many in Africa, Asia and South America.

Information Provided by Wikipedia
https://en.wikipedia.org/wiki/Child_support

Who Is the Attorney General?

In most common law jurisdictions, the **attorney general** or **attorney-general** is the main legal advisor to the government, and in some jurisdictions they may also have executive responsibility for law enforcement, prosecutions or even responsibility for legal affairs generally. In practice, the extent to which the attorney-general personally provides legal advice to the government varies between jurisdictions, and even between individual office-holders within the same jurisdiction, often depending on the level and nature of the office-holder's prior legal experience.

The term was originally used to refer to any person who holds a general power of attorney to represent a principal in all matters. In the common law tradition, anyone who represents the state, especially in criminal prosecutions, is such an attorney. Although a government may designate some official as the permanent attorney general, anyone who comes to represent the state in the same way may, in the past, be referred to as such, even if only for a particular case. Today, however, in most jurisdictions the term is largely reserved as a title of the permanently appointed attorney general of the state, sovereign or other member of the royal family. The term is pluralized attorneys general or attorneys-general.

Civil law jurisdictions have similar offices, who may be variously called "procurators", "advocates general", "public attorneys", and other titles. Many of these offices also use "attorney general" or "attorney-general" as the English translation of the title, although because of different historical provenance the nature of such offices is usually different from that of attorneys-general in common law jurisdictions.

In the federal government of the United States, the Attorney General is a member of the Cabinet and, as head of the Department of Justice, is the top law enforcement officer and lawyer for the government. The attorney general may need to be distinguished from the Solicitor General, a high Justice Department official with the responsibility of representing the government before the Supreme Court. In cases of exceptional importance, however, the Attorney General may choose personally to represent the government to the Supreme Court.

The individual U.S. states and territories, as well as the Federal capital of Washington, D.C., also have attorneys general with similar responsibilities. The majority of state Attorneys General are chosen by popular election, as opposed to the U.S. Attorney General, who is a presidential appointee confirmed by the Senate.

In nearly all United States jurisdictions the Attorney General is the chief law enforcement officer of that jurisdiction, and as such Attorney General may also be considered a police rank. The proper form of addressing a person holding the office of Attorney General is "Mister/Madam Attorney General," or "Attorney General," and referred to as "Attorney General." The shorthand form of address is "General." The plural is "Attorneys General" or "Attorneys-General". It is common in U.S. state governments that the state attorney general is addressed as "general." It is less commonplace that the federal attorney general is so addressed, though no less proper to do so.

Child Custody

Child custody and **legal-guardianship** are legal terms which are used to describe the legal and practical relationship between a parent and his or her child, such as the right of the child to make decisions and the parent's duty to care for the child.

Following ratification of the United Nations Convention on the Rights of the Child in most countries, terms such as "residence" and "contact" (known as "visitation" in the United States) have superseded the concepts of "custody" and "access". Instead of a parent having "custody" of or "access" to a child, a child is now said to "reside" or have "contact" with a parent. For a discussion of the new international nomenclature, see parental responsibility.

Residence and contact issues typically arise in proceedings involving divorce (dissolution of marriage), annulment, and other legal proceedings where children may be involved. In most jurisdictions the issue of which parent the child will reside with is determined in accordance with the best interests of the child standard.

Family law proceedings which involve issues of residence and contact often generate the most acrimonious disputes. While most parents cooperate when it comes to sharing their children and resort to mediation to settle a dispute, not all do. For those that engage in litigation, there seem to be few limits.

Court filings quickly fill with mutual accusations by one parent against the other, including sexual, physical, and emotional abuse, brain-washing, parental alienation syndrome, sabotage, and manipulation. It is these infrequent yet difficult custody battles that become public via the media and sometimes distort the public's perceptions so that the issues appear more prevalent than they are and the court's response appear inadequate.

Forum shopping to gain advantage occurs both between nations and where laws and practices differ between areas within a nation, The Hague Convention seeks to avoid this, also in the United States of America, the Uniform Child Custody Jurisdiction and Enforcement Act was adopted by all 50 states, family law courts were forced to defer jurisdiction to the home state.

In some places, courts and legal professionals are beginning to use the term parenting schedule instead of custody and visitation. The new terminology eliminates the distinction between custodial and noncustodial parents, and also attempts to build upon the best interests of the children by crafting schedules that meet the developmental needs of the children. For example, younger children need shorter, more frequent time with parents, whereas older children and teenagers may demand less frequent shifts yet longer blocks of time with each parent.

Forms of Custody

- Alternating custody is an arrangement whereby the child/children live for an extended period of time with one parent and an alternate amount of time with the other parent. While the child/children are with the parent, that parent retains sole authority and responsibility over the child/children. This type of arrangement is also referred to as Divided custody. [1]
- Shared custody[2] is an arrangement whereby the child/children live for an extended period of time with one parent, and then for a similar amount of time with the other parent. Opposite to alternating custody, both parents retain authority over the child/children.
- Bird's nest custody is an arrangement whereby the parents go back and forth from a residence in which the child/children reside, placing the burden of upheaval and movement on the parents rather than the child/children.
- Joint custody is an arrangement whereby both parents have legal custody and/or physical custody.
- Sole custody is an arrangement whereby only one parent has physical and legal custody of the child/children.
- Split custody is an arrangement whereby one parent has full-time custody over some children,

and the other parent has full custody over the other children.

- Third-party custody is an arrangement whereby the children do not remain with either biological parent, and are placed under the custody of a third person.

Physical Custody

Physical custody involves the day-to-day care of a child and establishes where a child will live. A parent with physical custody has the right to have his/her child live with him/her.

If a child lives with both parents, each parent shares "joint physical custody", and each parent is said to be a "custodial parent". Thus, in joint physical custody, neither parent is said to be a "non-custodial parent."[4] In joint physical custody, actual lodging and care of the child is shared according to a court-ordered custody schedule (also known as a "parenting plan" or "parenting schedule") In many cases, the term "visitation" is no longer used in this context, but rather is reserved to sole custody orders. Terms of art such as "primary custodial parent" and "primary residence" have no legal meaning other than for determining tax status, and both parents are still said to be "custodial parents".[5]

In some states, "joint physical custody" creates a presumption of "equal shared parenting". However, in most states, joint physical custody only creates an obligation to provide each of the parents with "significant periods" of physical custody so as to assure the child of "frequent and continuing contact" with both parents. Courts have not clearly defined what "significant periods" and "frequent and continuous contact" mean, which requires parents to litigate to find out.

If a child lives with one parent, that parent has "sole physical custody" and is said to be the "custodial parent" whereas the other parent is said to be the "non-custodial parent", but may have visitation rights or "visitation" with his/her child.

Joint physical custody

Joint physical custody is a court order whereby custody of a child is awarded to both parties. In joint custody, both parents are *custodial parents* and neither parent is a non-custodial parent; in other words, the child has two custodial parents.

Many states recognize two forms of joint custody: joint physical custody, and joint legal custody. In joint legal custody, both parents share the ability to have access to educational, health, and other records, and have equal decision-making status where the welfare of the child is concerned.

In joint physical custody, which would include joint physical care, actual lodging and care of the child is shared according to a court-ordered custody schedule (also known as a *parenting plan* or *parenting schedule*). In many cases, the term *visitation* is no longer used in these circumstances, but rather is reserved to sole custody orders.[7] In some states joint physical custody creates a presumption of equal shared parenting, however in most states, joint physical custody creates an obligation to provide each of the parents with "significant periods" of physical custody so as to assure the child of "frequent and continuing

156

contact" with both parents. For example, states such as Alabama, California, and Texas do not necessarily require joint custody orders to result in substantially equal parenting time, whereas states such as Arizona, Georgia, and Louisiana do require joint custody orders to result in substantially equal parenting time where feasible. Courts have not clearly defined what "significant periods" and "frequent and continuous contact" mean, which requires parents to litigate to find out.

It is important to note that joint physical custody and joint legal custody are different aspects of custody, and determination is often made separately in many states' divorce courts. E.g., it is possible to have joint legal custody, but for one parent to have sole physical custody In some states this is referred to as Custodial Parent and Non-Custodial Parent.

Also, where there is joint physical custody, terms of art such as "primary custodial parent" and "primary residence" have no legal meaning other than for determining tax status, and both parents are still custodial parents.

Sole physical custody

Sole physical custody means that a child shall reside with and be under the supervision of one parent, subject to the power of the court to order visitation. Physical custody involves the day-to-day care of a child and establishes where a child will live. A parent with physical custody has the right to have his/her child live with him/her. If a child lives with only one parent, that parent has *sole physical custody* and is said to be the *custodial parent*. The other parent is said to be the *non-custodial parent*, and may have visitation rights or *visitation* with his/her child.

Custodial parents

A *custodial parent* is a parent who is given physical and/or legal custody of a child by court order.

A *child-custody determination* means a judgment, decree, or other order of a court providing for the legal custody, physical custody, or visitation with respect to a child. The term includes a permanent, temporary, initial, and modification order. The term does not include an order relating to child support or other monetary obligation of an individual.[12] Where the child will live with both parents, joint physical custody is ordered, and both parents are custodial parents. Where the child will only live with one of the parents, sole physical custody is ordered, and the parent with which the child lives is the custodial parent, the other parent is the non-custodial parent.

Non-custodial parents

A *non-custodial parent* is a parent who does not have physical and/or legal custody of his/her child by court order.

A *child-custody determination* means a judgment, decree, or other order of a court providing for the legal custody, physical custody, or visitation with respect to a child. The term includes a permanent, temporary, initial, and modification order. The term does not include an order relating to child support or other monetary obligation of an individual.[12] Where the child will only live with one of the parents, sole physical custody is ordered, and the parent with which the child lives is the custodial parent, the other parent is the noncustodial parent. Note, however, where the child will live with both parents, joint physical custody is ordered, and both parent are custodial parents.

Information Provided by Wikipedia
https://en.wikipedia.org/wiki/Child_custody

The Child's Perspective

Mission Statement:

"Helping parents identify disagreements and communicate with understanding from The Child's emotional and psychological view".

As an effort to assist in raising awareness towards the issues that arise throughout co-parenting, Selfish Subjects, Inc. will be conducting events to raise funding for the 5013 non-profit organization The Child's Perspective.

If you would like more information on how you donate to this organization, please log on to www.thechildsperspective.com .

Special Thanks

We'd like to give a special thanks to our readers and supporters, as well as thank each and every parent and child that assisted in bringing this book to fruition. Your testimonial contributions will assist in our mission to bring awareness and understanding of the family matters embedded within these pages.